LOOPER
PEDAL SONGBOOK

50 Hits Arranged for Guitar
with Riffs, Chords, Lyrics & More

By Chad Johnson

ISBN 978-1-5400-1275-3

HAL•LEONARD®
7777 W. BLUEMOUND RD. P.O. BOX 13819 MILWAUKEE, WI 53213

Visit Hal Leonard Online at
www.halleonard.com

CONTENTS

INTRODUCTION

The looping craze has reached unthinkable heights over the past few years. Whereas once thought of as a bit of a novelty, looping pedals have become essential tools in many artists' gear lockers. Videos featuring loopers simply litter YouTube—from Michael Jackson covers to funky one-man improvs. Several name artists as well, including Ed Sheeran, KT Tunstall, Reggie Watts, Andrew Bird, and David Torn, among others, have made loopers an integral part of their live show, enabling them to create rich, dynamic, sprawling textures all by their lonesome. And yet, with all this popularity, very little in the way of loop-specific arrangements is available. Enter the *Looper Pedal Songbook*. In this book, you'll find 50 arrangements of songs in various styles that will put your looping skills to good use.

So, what is a looper anyway? In short, it's a device that stores musical phrases and plays them back for you. Not only that, but it allows you to overdub (or layer) new phrases on top of your original phrase. For example, you could record a bass line first, and then overdub some chords on top of it. Then you could record a melody or solo on top of the bass and chords, and then add a harmony to your melody or solo, and so on! Looping pedals come in many different varieties, but all of them will have this basic functionality. If you've not messed around with one much before, you're in for a world of musical fun! I hope you enjoy playing the arrangements in this book as much I did creating them.

ABOUT THE ARRANGEMENTS

Before we start laying down some grooves, we need to talk just a bit about equipment, conventions, and the terminology used in this book. After all, none of this has been standardized at this point, so I had to create a method of notating these concepts. After reading through this section, you should be well-equipped to understand anything you see in the following songs.

Assumptions

As each player's rig will differ substantially, it's important to clarify what's assumed with these arrangements. We've tried to aim for the lowest common denominator here, ensuring that the vast majority of players will be able to perform many of these arrangements "right out of the box." In other words, if you own a looper pedal, then you most likely own—or have access to—the rest of the gear mentioned. If not, however, there are still plenty of arrangements that can be performed with nothing but a guitar and a looper.

These arrangements have been designed to be performed on either an acoustic or electric guitar. Those designed for acoustic will say "Gtr. (acous.)" at the beginning of the song, and the electric ones will simply say "Gtr." at the beginning and give a tonal description, such as "w/ clean tone" or "w/ dist.," etc. The arrangements are therefore tailored to these instruments with regards to techniques. For example, many of the acoustic arrangements will feature percussive sounds that are often created by hitting various parts of the guitar's body. The electric arrangements will sometimes feature effects (such as delay, etc.) that are commonly employed with the electric guitar.

There are dozens of loopers on the market, from extremely simple to extremely sophisticated. The arrangements in this book should be performable on even the most modest looper. The only requirements are that:

- It's able to store loops of up to approximately 35 seconds—the longest loop called for is in the song "Sunny"

- It's able to endlessly overdub parts on top

- The loop can be turned on and off

- You are able to play "live" guitar parts on top while the loop is playing

I'm not aware of any loopers on the market that don't fit these criteria. In fact, most pedals will have many more features, such as multiple loops, an "undo" feature, etc. But the songs in this book have been arranged so that you won't need any of these fancier features.

Terminology

Let's take a look at the terms used in the book and what they mean.

Start Loop

This is usually the first direction you'll see. It instructs you to start recording a loop. For example, in many songs, you'll first start by laying down a bass line. Most of the arrangements only feature one loop during the song (though it may be turned off and turned back on later), so this direction will usually appear as "Start Loop 1." However, a few songs do feature an additional loop. In this instance, you'd need to clear the first loop (see your looper's manual) and start recording a new loop when you see "Start Loop 2."

End Loop

This is usually the second direction you'll see, and it tells you when to stop recording the loop. Once you do this, the loop should start playing back from the beginning. Again, you'll usually see this description as "End Loop 1."

Overdub on Loop

This tells you to start recording an overdub on top of your loop. In other words, if Loop 1 consists of a bass line, you may overdub some chords on top of it.

End Overdub

This tells you when to stop recording your overdub. The direction will usually coincide with the end of the looped phrase, but this is only because you'll usually be playing something right up until that point. If you only needed to overdub one note in the middle of the loop, there's no reason you couldn't stop overdubbing immediately after that note.

w/ Loop

This direction simply tells you that the loop should be playing. It's placed at the beginning of every new section of music in which the loop should be playing.

Loop Off

Occasionally, there will be times when you'll need to turn the loop off in a song. This is usually because the chord progression changes. Most times, this direction will appear at the end of the section immediately preceding the new one. For example, if the chord progression changes in the chorus, then you'll see "Loop 1 off" at the very end of the verse. Occasionally, however, due to certain routings, this direction may appear at the very beginning of the new section. In very few instances, it will appear in the middle of a section (or measure), in which case the turn-off point should be clear if you simply listen to the original recording of the song.

Loop On

If the loop has been turned off, this direction tells you to turn it back on. It will appear at the beginning of the new section where the loop returns. Note that this direction will only appear if the loop has been previously turned off. Otherwise, the "w/ Loop" direction will appear at any new section in which the loop is used.

Rhy. Fig.

This indicates the beginning of a rhythm part that will later be recalled. This is only used for "live" parts—i.e., parts that you (not the looper) will be playing more than once in the song. Most songs will use only one recalled rhythm figure, in which case it will be labeled "Rhy. Fig. 1." But a few songs will feature more than one.

End Rhy. Fig.

Working in conjuction with "Rhy. Fig.," this indicates the end of a rhythm part that will later be recalled. It will usually appear as "End Rhy. Fig. 1."

w/ Rhy. Fig.

This indicates that you should play the Rhy. Fig. that was identified earlier in the song. This is the "recall" of that figure. It's simply a means of saving space on the page.

Routing Directions

The common routing directions used in this book are as follows:

- **D.S. al Coda**: When you see this, return to the D.S. symbol (𝄋) and play until you see the "To Coda" indication. At that point, you jump to the Coda, which will be labeled with the (⊕) symbol, and continue on. Occasionally, a song will then reach a D.S.S. al Coda 2 direction. In this case, you'd go back to the D.S.S. sign (𝄋𝄋) and play until you see the "To Coda 2" indication. Then you'd jump to Coda 2 and continue on.

- **Bracketed Endings**: These are used with repeat signs. The first time you play through a section, you play through the first ending, which will be bracketed by a "1." When you hit the closed repeat sign, you go back to the open repeat sign and start again. This time, you skip over the first bracket and go to the second ending, which will be bracketed by a "2.," and continue on. Note that sometimes the first bracket should be played more than once, in which case it will bracketed with a "1., 2." or "1., 2., 3.," etc.

The music notated in this book uses **rhythm slashes** and/or **rhythm tab**. In the rhythm slash method, slashes are used to indicate the rhythms to be strummed. Whenever you see these slashes in a song, chord grids will appear at the beginning of the song to indicate which chord shapes/voicings to play. If you're unfamiliar with the rhythm tab method, check out the Rhythm Tab Legend at the back of the book for a thorough explanation.

Setting Up the Loop

For the majority of songs in this book, the process will be as follows: The first phrase played will be "Loop 1." This phrase will be surrounded by open and closed repeat signs, with "Start Loop 1" and "End Loop 1" appearing above these, respectively. This indicates that you will start recording on the looper, play the phrase—say, 4 bars long—stop recording on the looper, and then the looper will repeat the phrase for you. While the loop is playing, this gives you time to make any adjustments necessary (change effects/instrument settings, etc.) in order to get ready for the first overdub.

This process repeats as many times as necessary. In other words, the first overdubbed phrase will be surrounded by open and closed repeat signs, with "Overdub on Loop 1" and "End Overdub" appearing above these, respectively. Once the final overdub (for the time) has been completed, you'll move on to the next section, and you'll either see "w/ Loop 1," indicating that you should keep the loop playing, or "Loop 1 off," indicating that the loop should be turned off for the time being.

For many songs, such as "All Along the Watchtower," you'll create a fairly complete loop—maybe consisting of acoustic percussion (and/or bass) and chords—at the beginning and let it play through. This will allow you to focus on singing if you'd like, or adding fills if you prefer. If you'd rather play rhythm while you sing, then you can simply double the rhythm part or create your own complimentary part for a fuller sound. Often you'll have parts to play "live" over the loop later on, as well.

In some songs, however, such as "With or Without You," the loop will slowly build throughout the song. In other words, you'll create a loop, sing and/or play for a while, then overdub a new part onto the loop, then sing and/ or play for another section, then overdub another new part onto the loop, and so on. Still in other songs, such as "Ain't No Sunshine," you'll create a partial loop at first—maybe just the bass line—and then overdub the next layer of the loop (say, the chords) while singing the first verse.

All of these variations are possible, depending on several factors. These include:

- **The arrangement of the original recording**: Maybe the song starts with only drums and guitar, and the bass doesn't enter until later.

- **The logistics of equipment**: Certain parts may require more or less preparation.

- **The overall flow of the arrangement**: If we've spent a lot of time setting up the first loop, let's go ahead and get going with the verse, and overdub the last layer while the verse is being sung.

- **The logistics of when the vocals enter**: Do the vocals begin a few beats before the first verse?

- **Variety**: It's simply nice to mix it up sometimes.

A Word on Effects

Different effects are occasionally called for in the arrangements, and, while they will certainly help the arrangement resemble the original recording more, they should all be considered optional. All of the arrangements are still playable if you have nothing but your looper and guitar. Having said that, the effects called for will greatly enhance the arrangements.

By far, the most important effect to have (if you could only pick one) for the arrangements in this book is an octaver, also called an octave pedal. This effect will allow you to transpose your guitar down an octave, thereby enabling you to play a convincing bass line. This effect is called for in dozens of songs. However, you'll note that it's always preceded with "optional," indicating that you can still play the arrangement without it. It just won't have quite the same effect. Keep in mind that, if you do use an octave effect, be sure to turn it off before overdubbing the next part! (This direction always appears in the music to remind you.)

The other effects, such as delay, wah-wah, tremolo, chorus, etc., are generally less critical. Sometimes they're a bit more important than others—such as in "With or Without You," in which some of the guitar parts won't have the same sound without The Edge's signature dotted eighth-note delays—but for the most part, they're just enhancements to help you emulate the original recording.

Preparation

It's a good idea to look over an arrangement before diving in, as you may be required to make several different effects adjustments within the song. In other words, you may start with a clean tone, add a delay for the verse, turn off the delay and add distortion for the chorus, etc. Therefore, it's a good idea to know what's coming up in this regard.

If you have a multi-effects unit—which I would recommend when playing looper arrangements simply because of the versatility—then you can set up a batch of presets all dedicated to one song. By doing this, you could keep them in order and simply step through the presets as necessary as you progress through the song.

Experimentation and Malleability

Having said all of this, please realize that these arrangements should not be thought of as set in stone. You can feel free to experiment, especially if your rig allows for more options. For example, if you have a looper that's able to store multiple loops, then you could assign the bass line to one loop, the percussion to another, and the chords to yet another. This way, even if you had to turn off the bass and chords loop and play some chords "live" for a new section, you could keep the percussion loop playing underneath.

Or maybe your rig includes a drum pad to trigger drum samples, or you have real percussion instruments—such as a shaker, cajon, etc.—that you can mic up. You may want to substitute those percussion sounds instead of using the ones notated here. And speaking of percussion sounds, keep in mind that I've notated acoustic guitar percussion sounds in a way that works for me, but if you want to simulate these sounds in another way, that's great. I always indicated with a footnote what was being simulated, so feel free to use whichever method works best for you.

This book doesn't cover the subject of using the looper with vocals (or with a mic, period) at all, but that's certainly another option with regards to adding vocal harmonies, melodies, or percussion (produced either with your mouth or by miking a drum). This will certainly increase the possibilities in all regards.

Finally, you should feel free to mix and match instruments as your rig affords. For example, if you make it a habit to have an actual bass on stage with you in addition to your guitar, then feel free to use it instead of using an octaver on the guitar. Or if your rig includes both acoustic and electric guitars, then feel free to mix and match them as you see fit. A good example of this is "Wicked Game." Although the rhythmic bed is provided by an acoustic guitar (and the arrangement here is therefore designed for acoustic), the song's signature guitar riff, which appears after the chorus, is played on electric on the original recording, so you could switch to electric at that point if you desire.

Of course, guitars, basses, and percussion aren't the only options either. If you have a banjo, violin, mandolin, trumpet, synth, etc. in your rig, and you aren't afraid to use it, you could add one or all of them to any of the songs as you see fit. As mentioned earlier, this book assumes a lowest common denominator to make it as accessible as possible, but if you want to expand on these arrangements in any way, there's plenty of room! Most of all, have fun with these arrangements.

Ok, that's enough blabbering. Ladies and gentlemen … start your loopers!

Ain't No Sunshine

Words and Music by Bill Withers

Key of Am
Intro
  Moderately slow

2nd time: 1. Ain't no sun - shine when she's

N.C. (Am)

Gtr.   **Start Loop 1**   **End Loop 1**

w/ clean tone
w/ fingers

Optional: w/ octaver set for one octave below.

Verse

gone.   It's not warm when she's a -
2., 3. *See additional lyrics*

Am7   Em7   G7   Am7

Overdub on Loop 1   **End Overdub**

Octaver off

w/ Loop 1   **Loop 1 off**

                    Em7   G7   Am7

way.   Ain't no sun - shine when she's gone,

and she's al - ways gone too long   an - y - time   she goes a -

Em7   Dm7

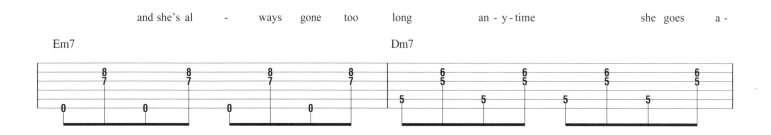

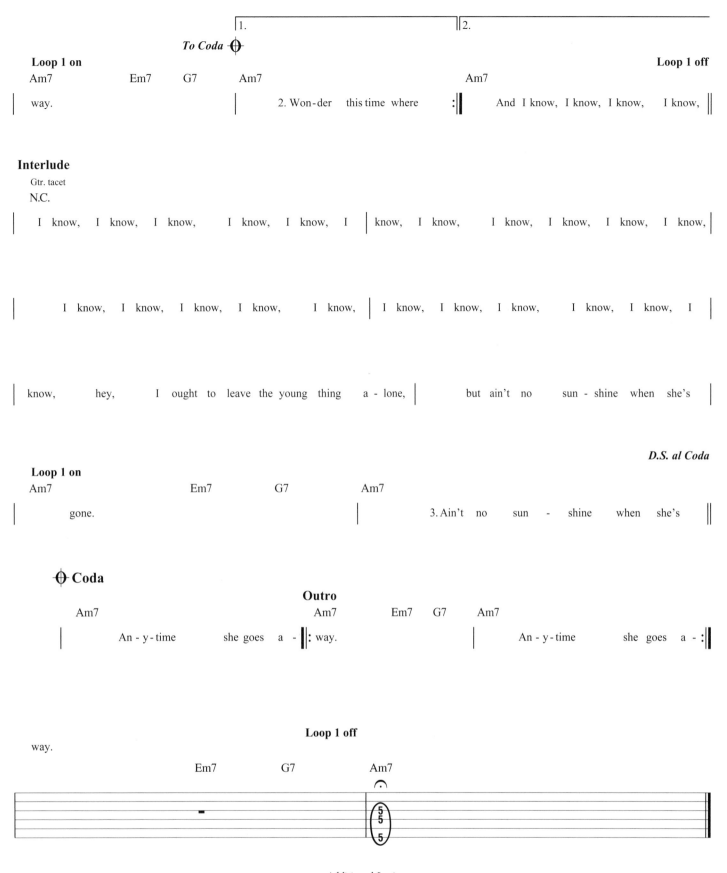

All Along the Watchtower

Words and Music by Bob Dylan

Capo II
Key of C#m (Capo key of Bm)
Intro
Moderately

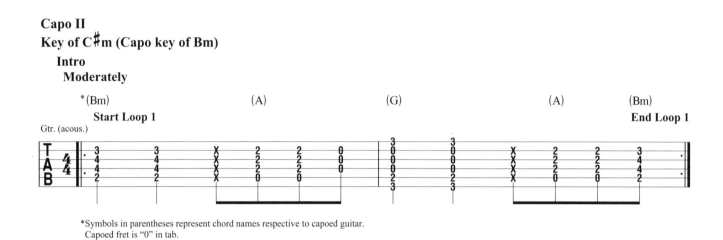

*Symbols in parentheses represent chord names respective to capoed guitar.
Capoed fret is "0" in tab.

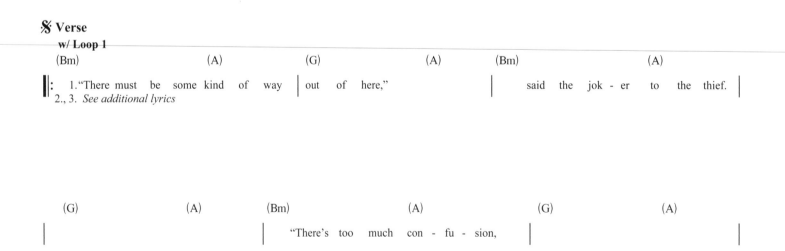

Overdub on Loop 1

End Overdub

**Slap body of gtr. w/ right hand to produce kick & snare percussion effect.

𝄋 Verse
w/ Loop 1

(Bm)   (A)   (G)   (A)   (Bm)   (A)

1. "There must be some kind of way | out of here," | said the jok-er to the thief.
2., 3. *See additional lyrics*

(G)   (A)   (Bm)   (A)   (G)   (A)

"There's too much con-fu-sion,

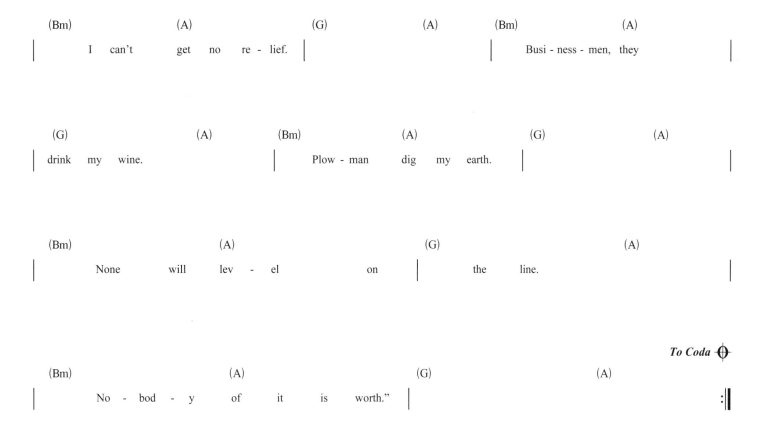

(Bm)   (A)   (G)   (A)   (Bm)   (A)

I   can't   get   no   re - lief.   Busi - ness - men, they

(G)   (A)   (Bm)   (A)   (G)   (A)

drink   my   wine.   Plow - man   dig   my   earth.

(Bm)   (A)   (G)   (A)

None   will   lev - el   on   the   line.

To Coda ⊕

(Bm)   (A)   (G)   (A)

No - bod - y   of   it   is   worth."

Interlude
w/ Loop 1

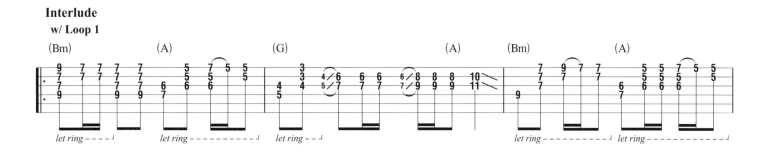

(Bm)   (A)   (G)   (A)   (Bm)   (A)

let ring   *let ring*   *let ring*   *let ring*   *let ring*

2nd time, D.S. al Coda   ⊕ **Coda**

Loop 1 off

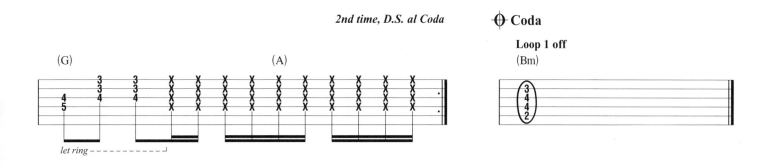

(G)   (A)   (Bm)

let ring

Additional Lyrics

2. "No reason to get excited," the thief, he kindly spoke.
   "There are many here among us who feel that life is but a joke.
   But you and I, we've been through that, and this is not our fate.
   So let us not talk falsely now; the hour's getting late."

3. All along the watchtower, princes kept the view.
   While all the women came and went, barefoot servants, too.
   Outside in the cold distance, a wildcat did growl.
   Two riders were approaching, and the wind began to howl.

Billie Jean

Words and Music by Michael Jackson

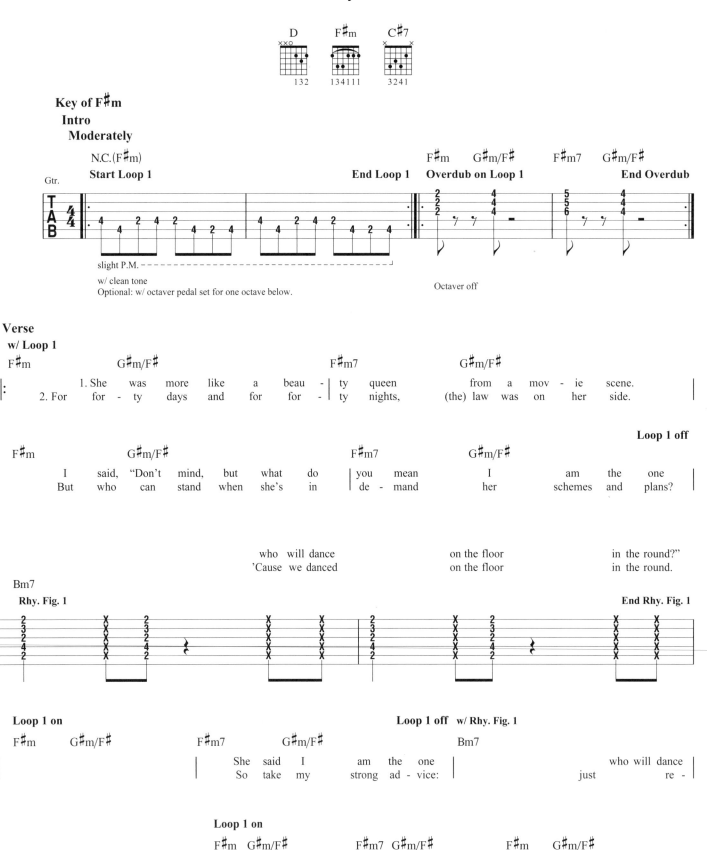

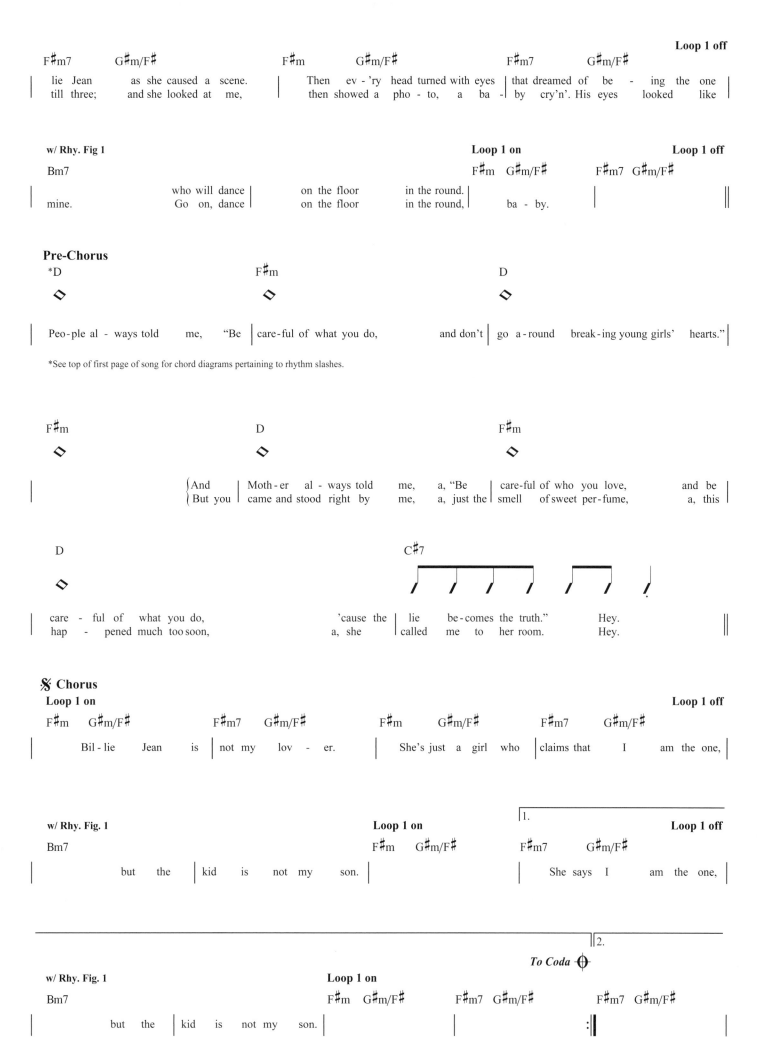

F#m   G#m/F#   F#m7   G#m/F#   F#m   G#m/F#   F#m7   G#m/F#

| Bil - lie   Jean   is | not my   lov - er. | She's just a girl who | claims that   I   am the one, |

w/ Rhy. Fig. 1   Loop 1 on   Loop 1 off

Bm7   F#m   G#m/F#   F#m7   G#m/F#

| but the | kid   is   not my   son. | | She says I   am the one, |

w/ Rhy. Fig. 1   Loop 1 on

Bm7   F#m   G#m/F#   F#m7   G#m/F#

| but the | kid   is   not my   son. | | ‖

Interlude
w/ Loop 1

F#m   G#m/F#   F#m7   G#m/F#   F#m   G#m/F#

Rhy. Fig. 2

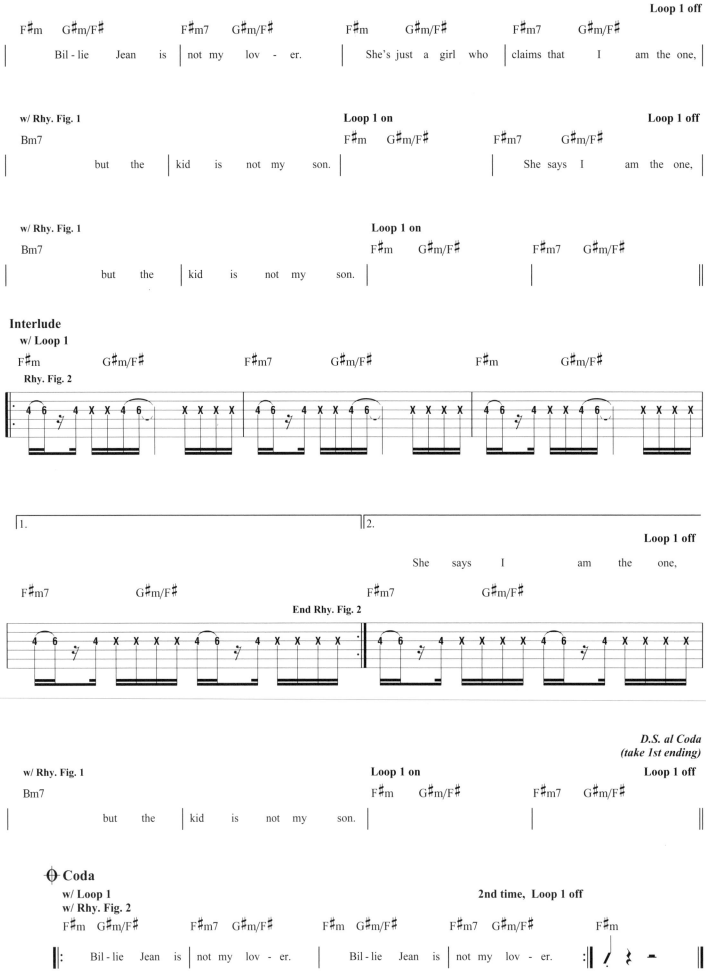

1.   2.

Loop 1 off

She   says   I   am   the   one,

F#m7   G#m/F#   F#m7   G#m/F#

End Rhy. Fig. 2

D.S. al Coda
(take 1st ending)

w/ Rhy. Fig. 1   Loop 1 on   Loop 1 off

Bm7   F#m   G#m/F#   F#m7   G#m/F#

| but the | kid   is   not my   son. | | ‖

⊕ Coda
w/ Loop 1   2nd time, Loop 1 off
w/ Rhy. Fig. 2

F#m G#m/F#   F#m7 G#m/F#   F#m G#m/F#   F#m7 G#m/F#   F#m

‖: Bil - lie Jean is | not my lov - er. | Bil - lie Jean is | not my lov - er. :‖

Black Horse and the Cherry Tree

Words and Music by Katie Tunstall

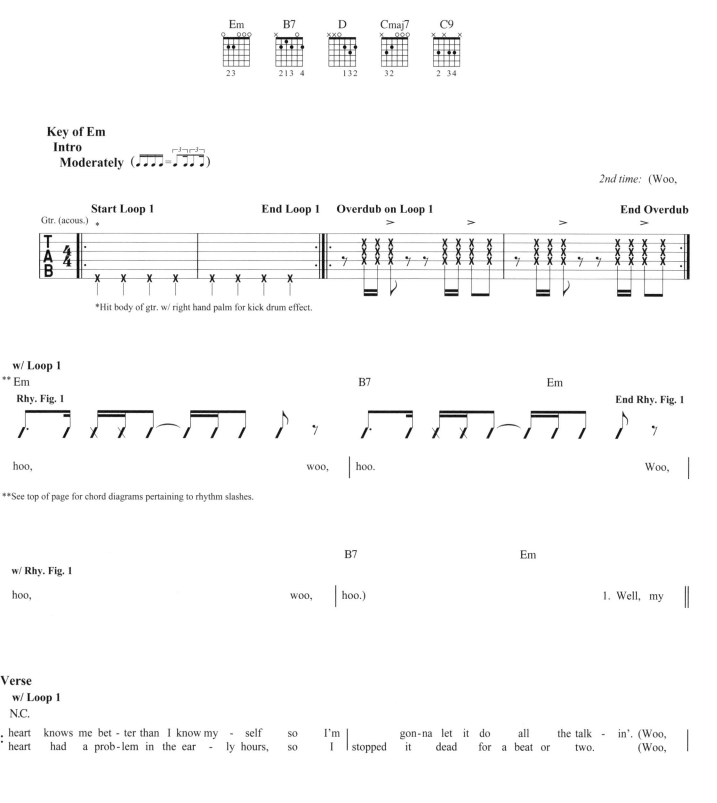

Key of Em
Intro
Moderately

2nd time: (Woo,

Start Loop 1   **End Loop 1**   **Overdub on Loop 1**   **End Overdub**

Gtr. (acous.)

*Hit body of gtr. w/ right hand palm for kick drum effect.

w/ Loop 1
Em   **B7**   **Em**
Rhy. Fig. 1   **End Rhy. Fig. 1**

hoo,   woo, | hoo.   Woo,

**See top of page for chord diagrams pertaining to rhythm slashes.

                                        B7   **Em**
w/ Rhy. Fig. 1
hoo,   woo, | hoo.)   1. Well, my

Verse
w/ Loop 1
N.C.

heart knows me bet-ter than I know my-self so I'm | gon-na let it do all the talk-in'. (Woo,
heart had a prob-lem in the ear-ly hours, so I | stopped it dead for a beat or two.   (Woo,

w/ Rhy. Fig. 1
Em   **B7**   **Em**
hoo,   woo, | hoo.)   I
hoo,   woo, | hoo.)   But I

N.C.

| came a-cross a place in the mid-dle of no-where with a | big, black horse and a cher-ry tree. (Woo, |
| cut some cord and I should-n't have done that, and it | won't for-give me af-ter all these years. (Woo, |

w/ Rhy. Fig. 1

Em · · · B7 · Em

| hoo, woo, | hoo.) I |
| hoo, woo, | hoo.) So I |

N.C.

| fell in fear up-on my back I said, | "Don't look back, just keep on walk-ing." (Woo, |
| sent her to a place in the mid-dle of no-where with a | big, black horse and a cher-ry tree. (Woo, |

w/ Rhy. Fig. 1

Em · · · B7 · Em

| hoo, woo, | hoo.) When the big |
| hoo, woo, | hoo.) Now it |

N.C.

| black horse that looked this way said | "Hey, la-dy, will you mar-ry me?" (Woo, |
| won't come back 'cause it's oh, so hap-py and now | I got a hole for the world to see. (Woo, |

w/ Rhy. Fig. 1

Em · · · B7 · Em

| hoo, woo, | hoo.) But I said, |
| hoo, woo, | hoo.) And it said, |

Chorus

w/ Loop 1

Em · · · D · · · Cmaj7

Rhy. Fig. 2

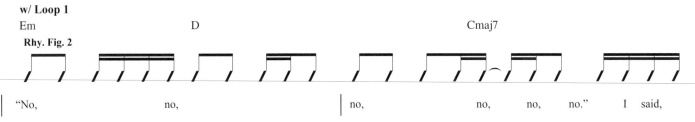

| "No, no, | no, no, no, no." I said, |

Em · D · C9 · · · Em · · · D

| "No, no, you're | not the one for me. No, no, |

Cmaj7 · · · Em · · · D

End Rhy. Fig. 2

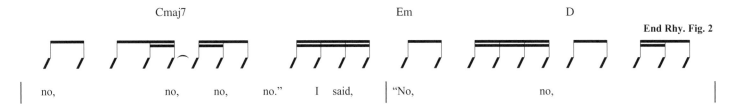

| no, no, no, no." I said, | "No, no, |

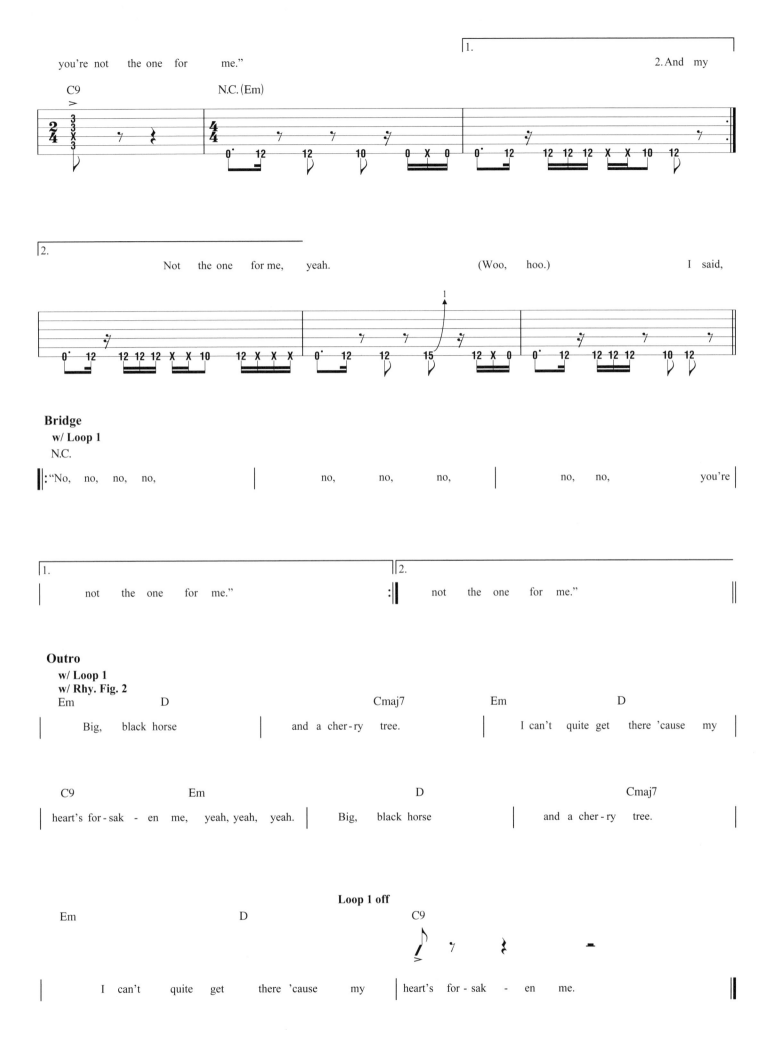

you're not the one for   me."

2. And my

C9

N.C. (Em)

2.

Not   the one   for me,   yeah.

(Woo,   hoo.)

I said,

Bridge
w/ Loop 1
N.C.

:"No, no, no, no,

no,   no,   no,

no, no,   you're

1.

not   the one   for me."

2.

not   the one   for me."

Outro
w/ Loop 1
w/ Rhy. Fig. 2

Em	D	Cmaj7	Em	D

Big,   black horse

and a cher-ry tree.

I can't quite get   there 'cause   my

C9	Em	D	Cmaj7

heart's for-sak - en me, yeah, yeah, yeah.

Big,   black horse

and a cher-ry tree.

Loop 1 off

Em	D	C9

I can't   quite get   there 'cause   my

heart's for-sak - en me.

Born on the Bayou

Words and Music by John Fogerty

Key of E
Intro
Moderately

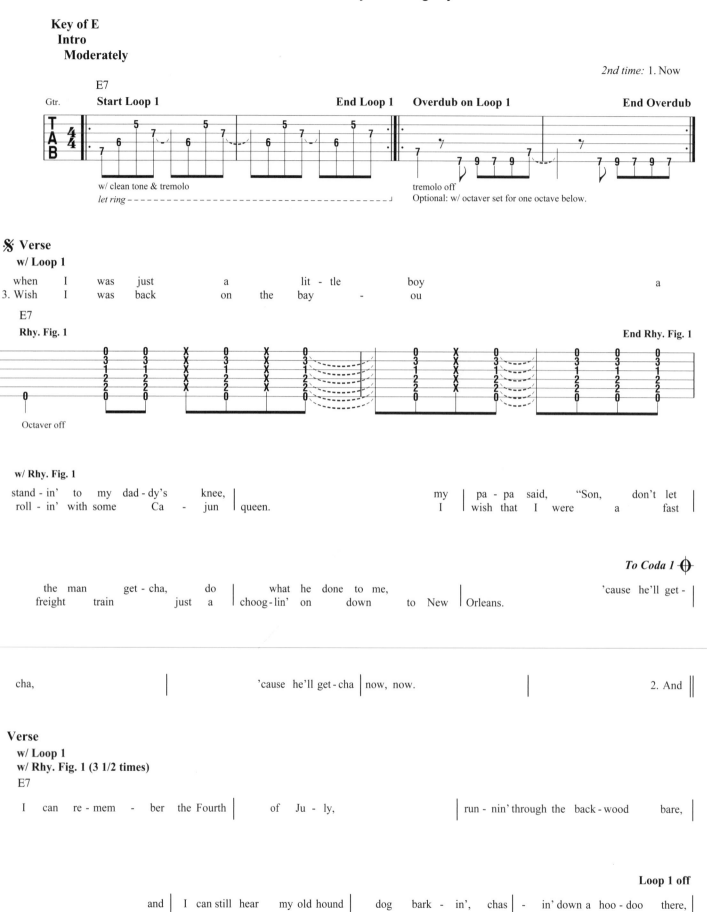

2nd time: 1. Now

when I was just a lit - tle boy a
3. Wish I was back on the bay - ou

stand - in' to my dad - dy's knee, my pa - pa said, "Son, don't let
roll - in' with some Ca - jun queen. I wish that I were a fast

To Coda 1

the man get - cha, do what he done to me, 'cause he'll get -
freight train just a choog - lin' on down to New Orleans.

cha, 'cause he'll get - cha now, now. 2. And

Verse
w/ Loop 1
w/ Rhy. Fig. 1 (3 1/2 times)
E7

I can re - mem - ber the Fourth of Ju - ly, run - nin' through the back - wood bare,

Loop 1 off

and I can still hear my old hound dog bark - in', chas - in' down a hoo - doo there,

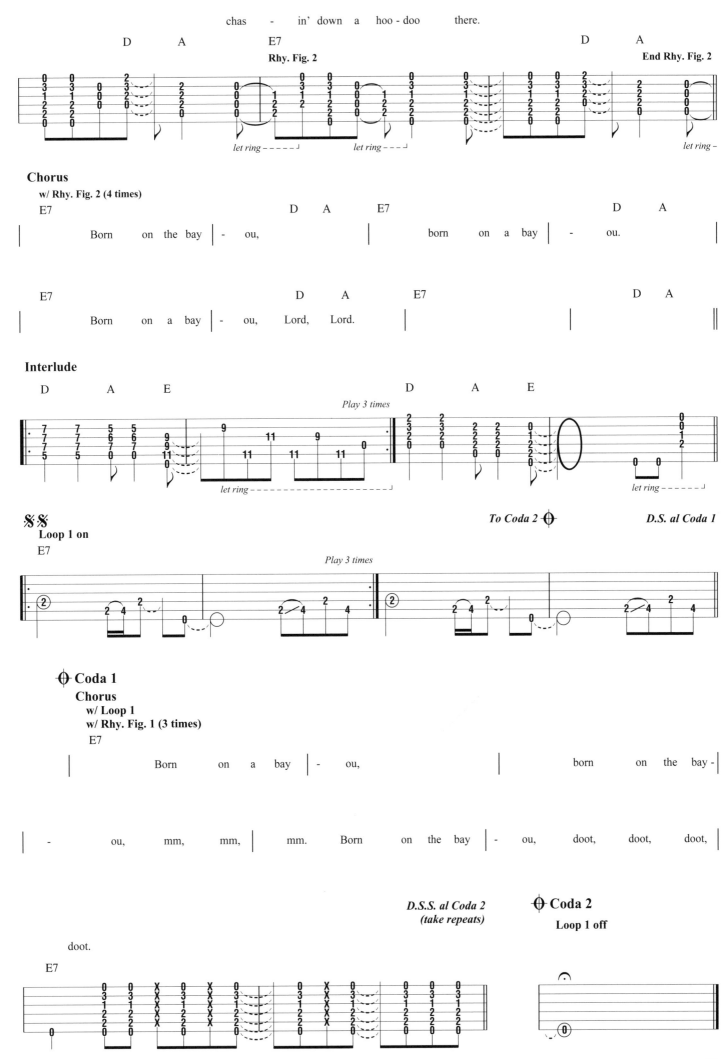

chas - in' down a hoo - doo there.

Chorus
w/ Rhy. Fig. 2 (4 times)

Born on the bay - ou, born on a bay - ou.

Born on a bay - ou, Lord, Lord.

Interlude

Born on a bay - ou, born on the bay -

- ou, mm, mm, mm. Born on the bay - ou, doot, doot, doot,

doot.

Brain Stew

Words by Billie Joe Armstrong
Music by Green Day

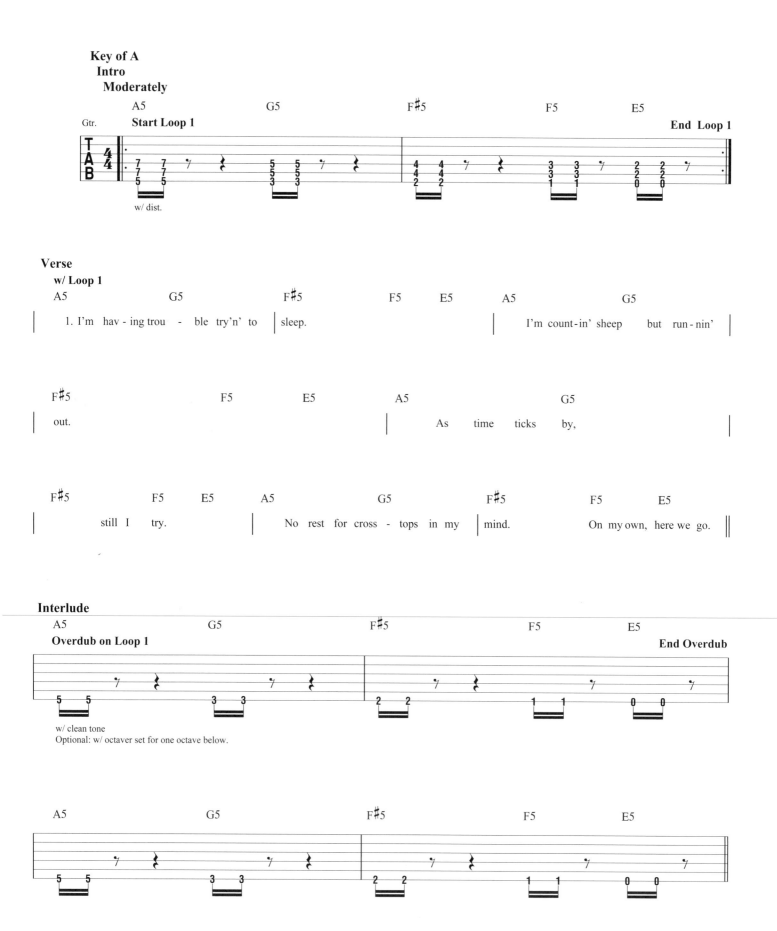

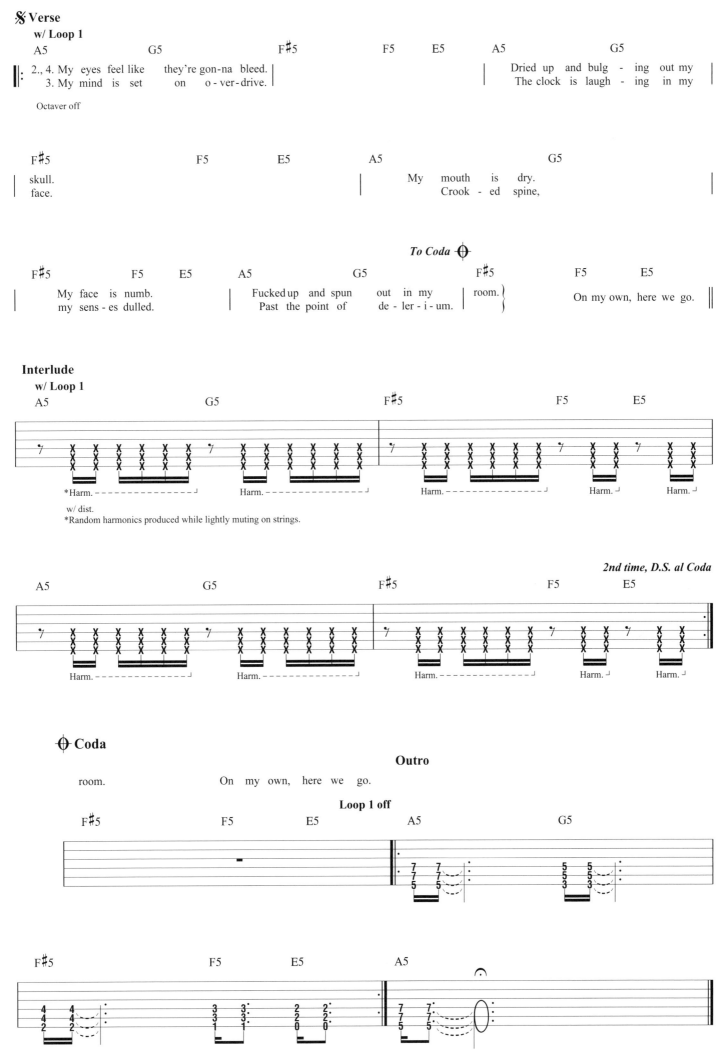

Brick House

Words and Music by Lionel Richie, Ronald LaPread, Walter Orange, Milan Williams, Thomas McClary and William King

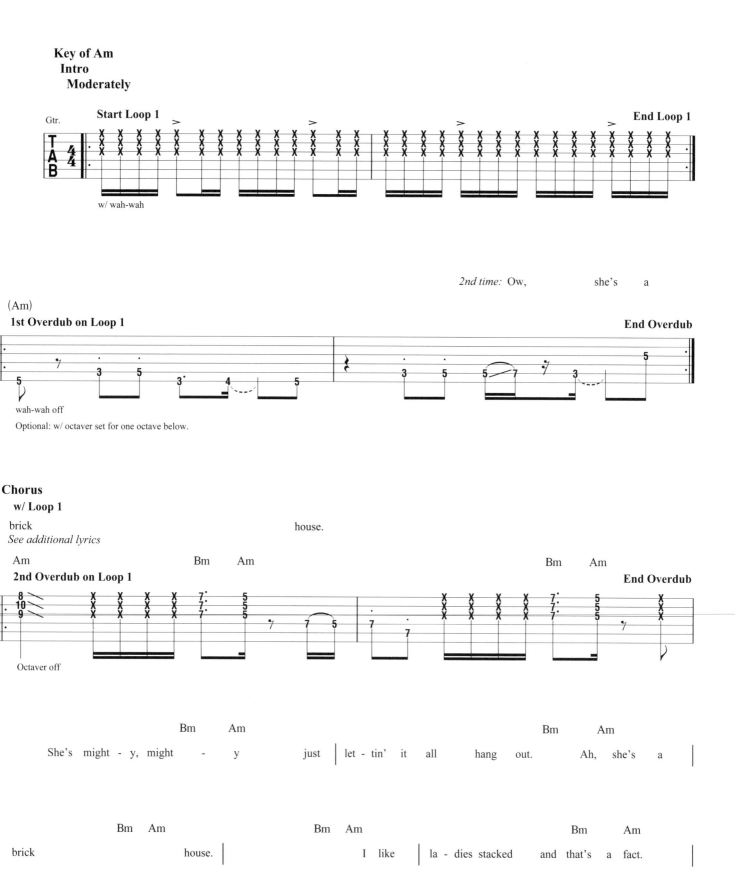

Bm   Am   Bm   Am   Bm   Am

Ain't hold-in' no-thin' back. Ow, she's a | brick   house. |

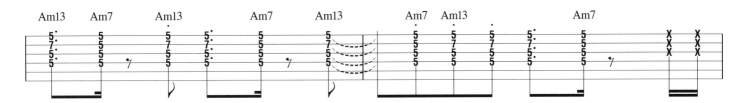

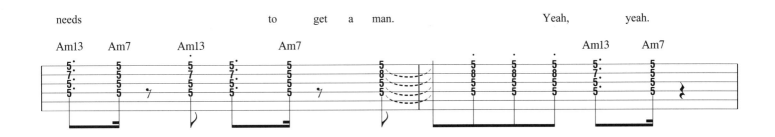

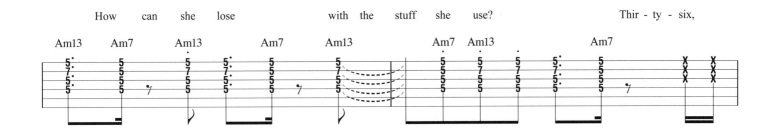

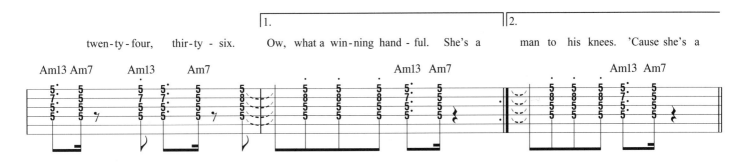

𝄋 Chorus

Loop 1 on

Am — Bm Am — Bm Am — Bm Am

| brick house. | Yeah, she's might - y, might - y just |

Bm Am — Bm Am — Bm Am

| let - tin' it all hang out. Hey, | brick house. | I like / Yeah, |

To Coda ⊕

1st time, Loop 1 off

Bm Am — Bm Am

| la - dies stacked and that's a fact. | Ain't hold - in' noth - in' back. Ow. |
| she's the one, the on - ly one, | built like an Am - a - zon. |

Bridge

A shake it down, shake it down now.   A shake it down, shake it down now.

Am11

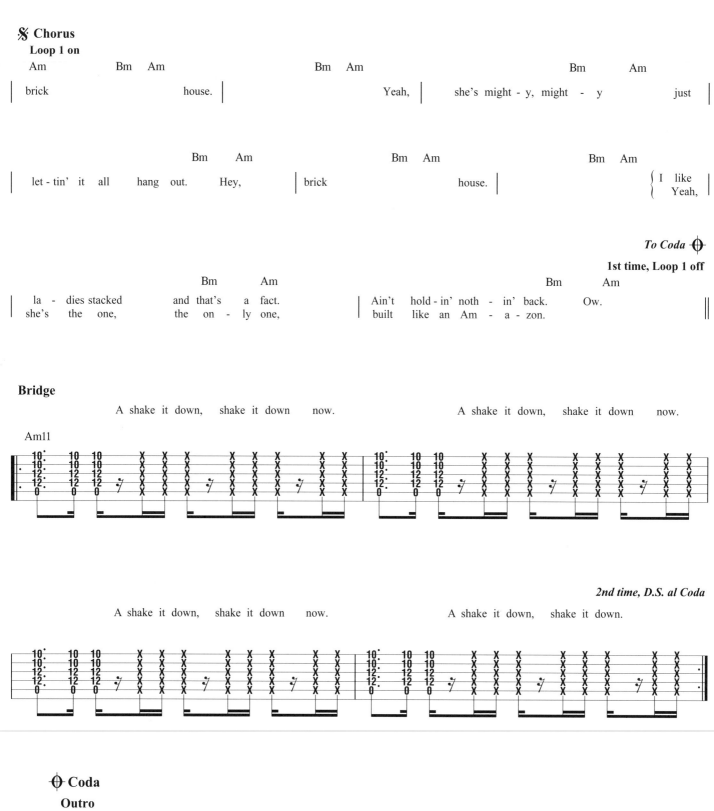

2nd time, D.S. al Coda

A shake it down, shake it down now.   A shake it down, shake it down.

⊕ Coda

Outro

w/ Loop 1   **4th time, Loop 1 off**

Brick   house.

Am — Bm Am — Bm Am

Play 4 times

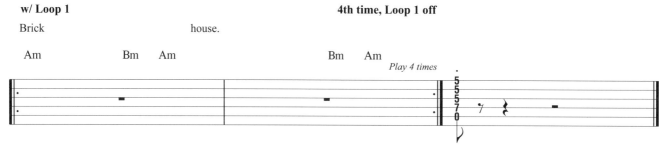

Additional Lyrics

2. Mm, the clothes she wear, her sexy ways
   Make an old man wish for younger days, yeah, yeah.
   She knows she's built and knows how to please.
   Sure 'nough can knock a strong man to his knees.

Dosed

Words and Music by Anthony Kiedis, Flea, John Frusciante and Chad Smith

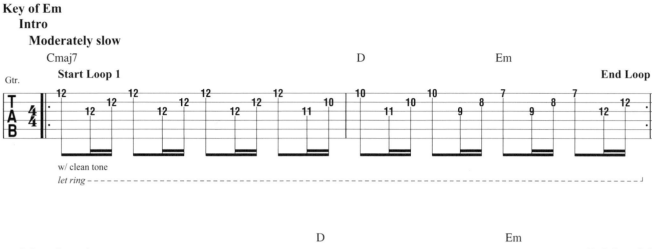

Key of Em
Intro
Moderately slow

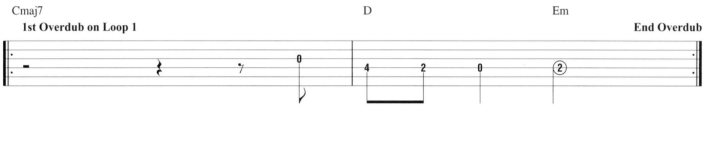

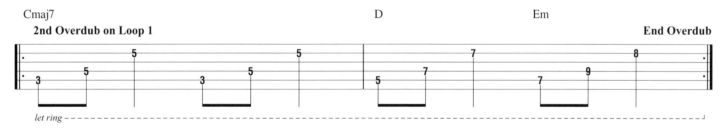

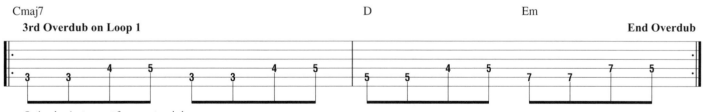

Optional: w/ octaver set for one octave below.

Verse
w/ Loop 1

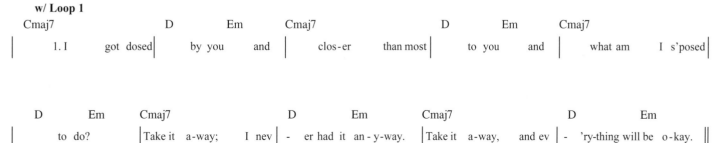

Cmaj7	D	Em	Cmaj7	D	Em	Cmaj7
1. I got dosed	by you	and	clos-er than most	to you	and	what am I s'posed

D	Em	Cmaj7	D	Em	Cmaj7	D	Em
to do?	Take it a-way; I nev	- er had it an-y-way.	Take it a-way,	and ev	- 'ry-thing will be o-kay.

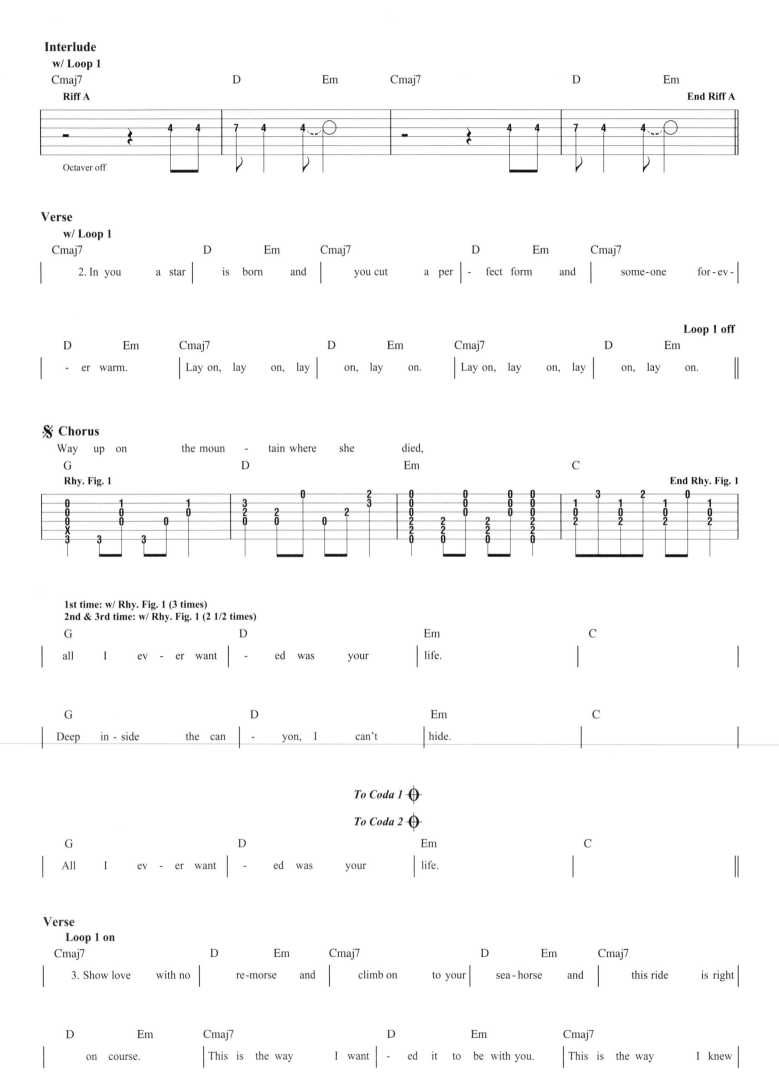

D	Em	Cmaj7		D	Em	Cmaj7		D	Em	
that it would be with you.	Lay on, lay	on, lay	on, lay on.	Lay on, lay	on, lay	on, lay on.	

⊕ **Coda 1**

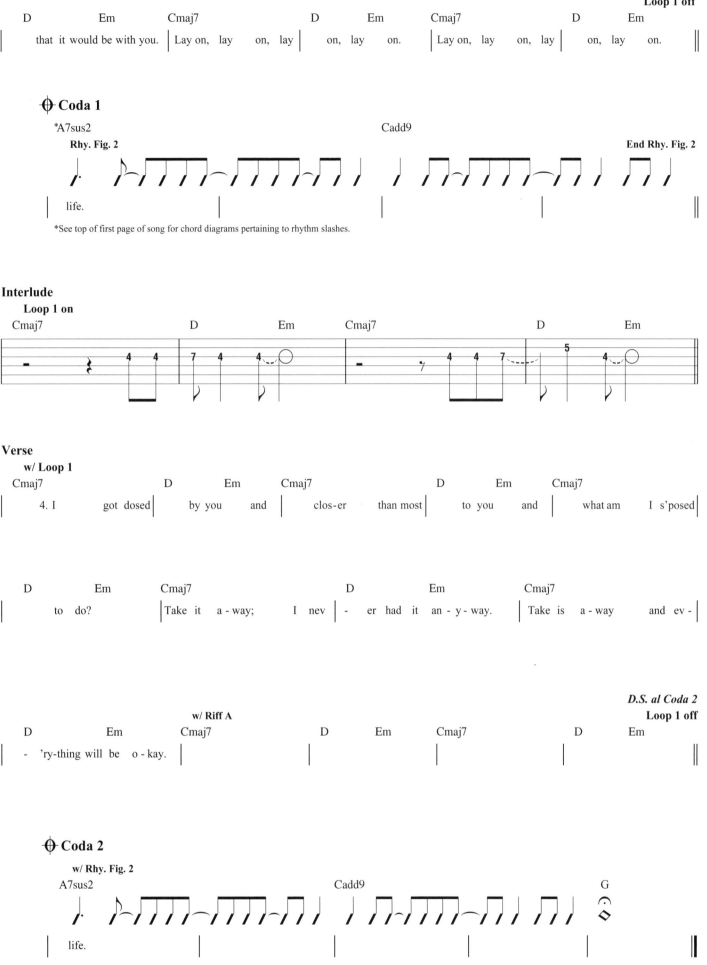

*See top of first page of song for chord diagrams pertaining to rhythm slashes.

Interlude
Loop 1 on

Verse
w/ Loop 1

Cmaj7		D	Em	Cmaj7		D	Em	Cmaj7	
4. I	got dosed	by you	and	clos-er	than most	to you	and	what am	I s'posed

D		Em	Cmaj7			D		Em	Cmaj7	
to do?		Take it a-way;	I nev	-	er had it an-y-way.	Take is a-way		and ev-

w/ Riff A

D	Em	Cmaj7		D	Em	Cmaj7		D	Em	
- 'ry-thing will be o-kay.			

⊕ **Coda 2**
w/ Rhy. Fig. 2

life.

Chain of Fools

Words and Music by Don Covay

Key of Cm
Intro
Moderately

2nd time: Chain, chain, chain.

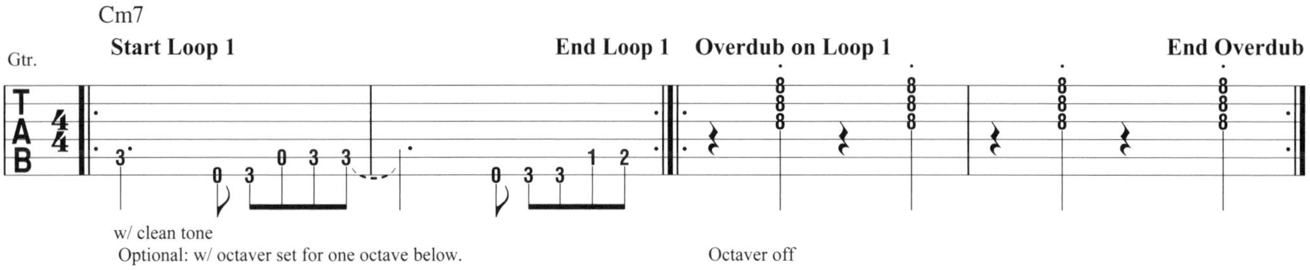

Cm7

Gtr.

Start Loop 1   **End Loop 1**   **Overdub on Loop 1**   **End Overdub**

w/ clean tone
Optional: w/ octaver set for one octave below.

Octaver off

% Chorus
w/ Loop 1
Cm7

(Chain, chain, chain.)   Chain, chain, chain.   (Chain, chain, chain.)   Chain, chain, chain.

(Chain, chain, chain.)   Chain of fools.   1. For five long years
3. One of these morn-

Verse
w/ Loop 1
Cm7

- ings,   I thought you   were my man.   But I found
the chain is   gon - na break.   But up un - til

To Coda ⊕

out   I'm just a link in your chain.   Oh.   You got me where you
then, yeah,   I'm gon - na take all I can take.   Oh.

want me,   I ain't noth - ing but your fool.   You treat - ed me mean,

oh,   you treat - ed me cruel.   Chain, chain, chain.

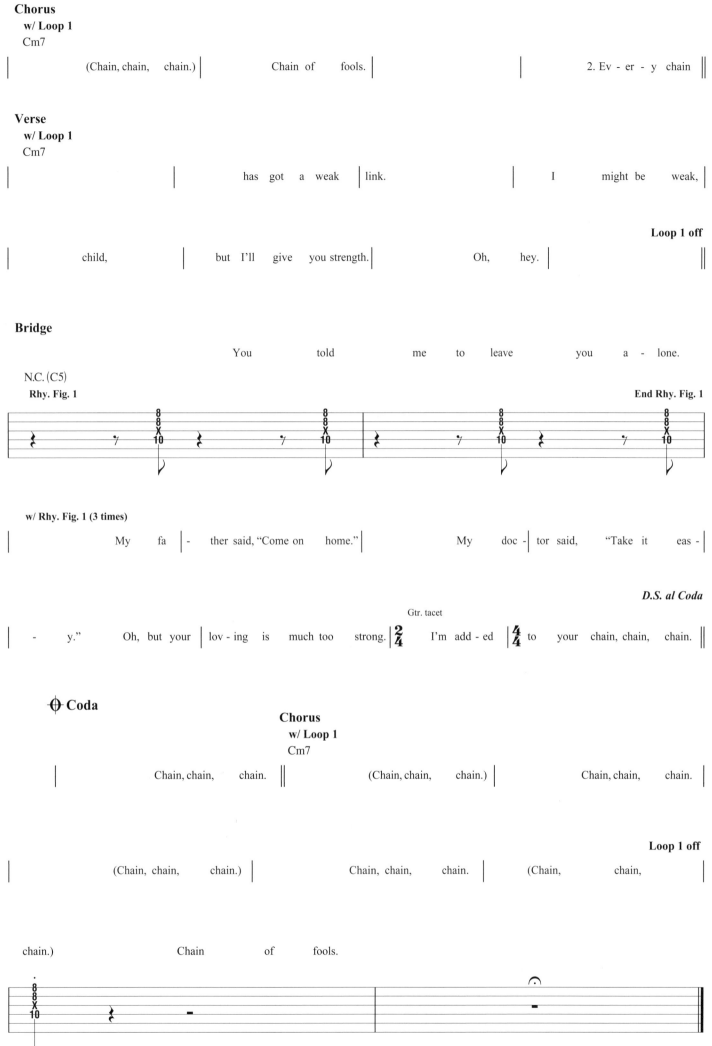

Chorus
w/ Loop 1
Cm7

(Chain, chain, chain.)   Chain of   fools.   2. Ev - er - y chain

Verse
w/ Loop 1
Cm7

has got a weak link.   I   might be   weak,

Loop 1 off

child,   but I'll give   you strength.   Oh,   hey.

Bridge

You   told   me   to   leave   you   a - lone.

N.C. (C5)
Rhy. Fig. 1   **End Rhy. Fig. 1**

w/ Rhy. Fig. 1 (3 times)

My   fa   - ther said, "Come on   home."   My   doc - tor said,   "Take it   eas -

D.S. al Coda

Gtr. tacet

- y."   Oh, but your lov - ing is much too strong. **2/4**   I'm add - ed **4/4** to   your chain, chain, chain.

Coda

Chorus
w/ Loop 1
Cm7

Chain, chain,   chain.   (Chain, chain,   chain.)   Chain, chain,   chain.

Loop 1 off

(Chain, chain,   chain.)   Chain, chain,   chain.   (Chain,   chain,

chain.)   Chain   of   fools.

Chasing Cars

Words and Music by Gary Lightbody, Tom Simpson, Paul Wilson, Jonathan Quinn and Nathan Connolly

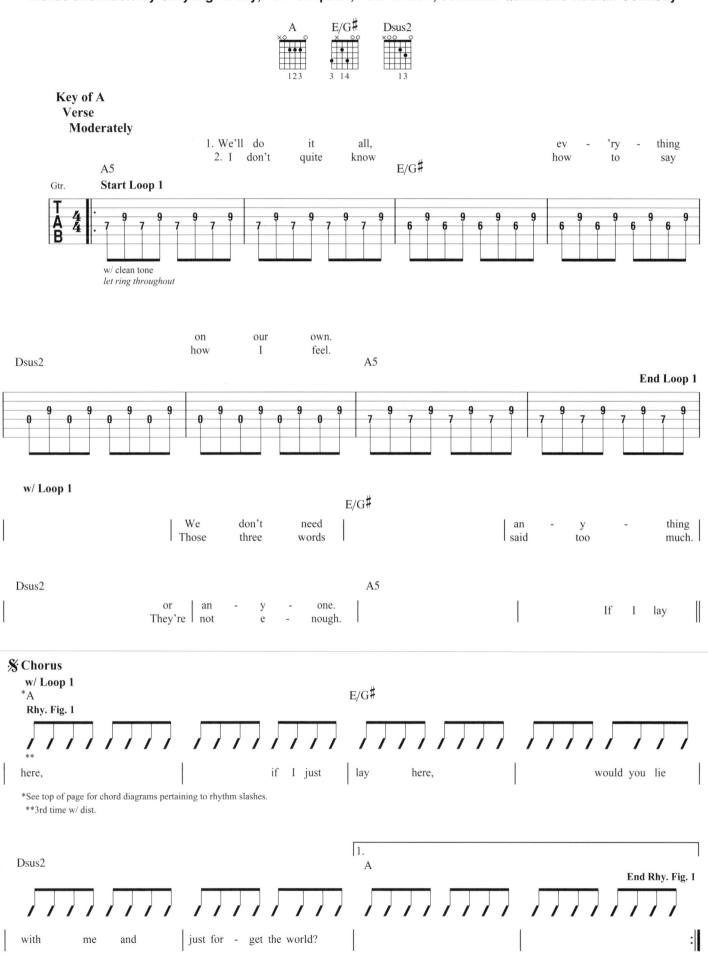

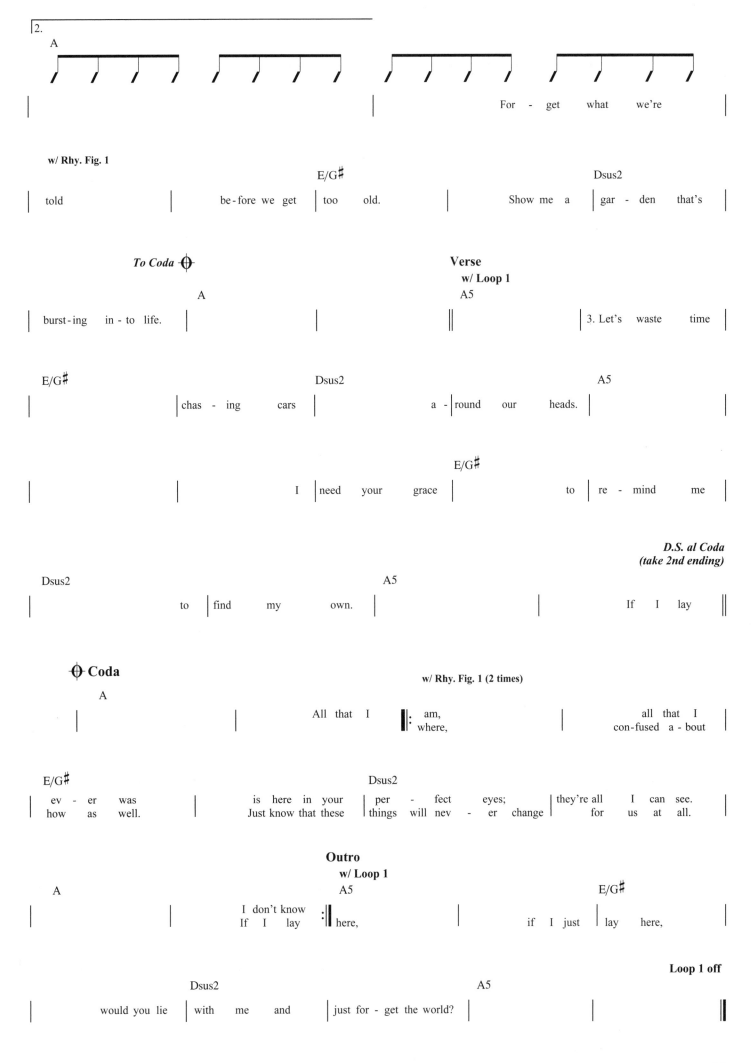

Creep

Words and Music by Albert Hammond, Mike Hazlewood, Thomas Yorke, Jonathan Greenwood, Colin Greenwood, Edward O'Brien and Philip Selway

G

Key of G
Intro
    Moderately slow

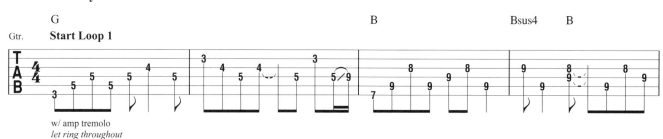

Gtr.   **Start Loop 1**

w/ amp tremolo
let ring throughout

1. When you were here be-fore,

End Loop 1

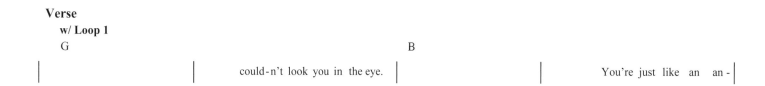

Verse
  w/ Loop 1

G   could-n't look you in the eye.   B   You're just like an an-

C   - gel.   Your skin makes me cry.   Cm

You float like a feath - er   G   in a beau-ti-ful world.   B

I wish I was spe - cial.   C   You're so fuck-ing spe-

- cial,   but I'm a   creep.

Cm

%‍ **Chorus**

w/ Loop 1

I'm a weird - o.   What the hell am I do - ing here?

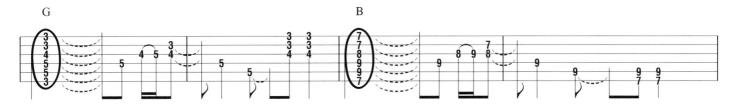

To Coda ⊕

I don't be - long   here.

Verse

w/ Loop 1

2. I don't care if it hurts,   I wan - na have con - trol.

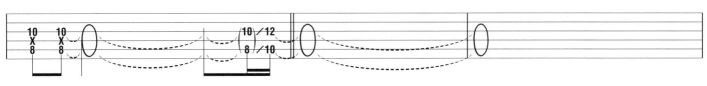

I want a per - fect bod|- y.

I want a per - fect soul.   I want you to no |- tice

B

when I'm   not   a - round. | You're so fuck - ing spe -

D.S. al Coda

w/ Rhy. Fig. 1

C   Cm

- cial. | I   wish I   was spe |- cial, | but I'm a   creep. ‖

⊕ Coda

here. | Oh. | Oh.

Cm

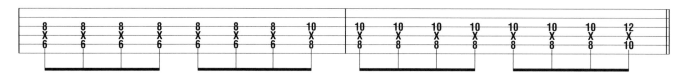

Bridge

w/ Loop 1

She's | run - ning out | a - gain.

G   B

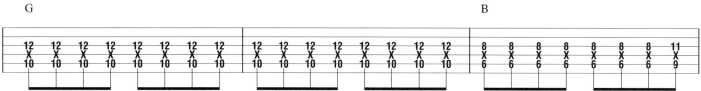

She's | run - ning out. | She

C

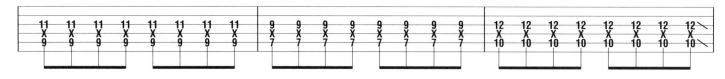

run, | run, | run, | run.

Cm   G

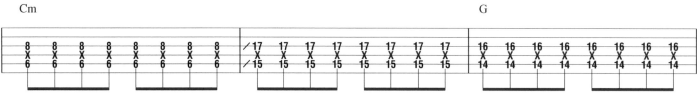

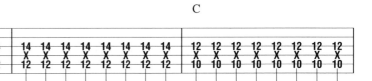

Run.

3. What - ev - er makes you hap -

Verse
w/ Loop 1

G

\- py. What - ev - er you want. You're so fuck - ing spe -

B

C

\- cial. I wish I was spe - cial, but I'm a creep.

Cm

Outro-Chorus
w/ Loop 1

G

I'm a weird - o.

B

What the hell am I do - ing here? I don't be - long

C

Loop 1 off
*G

Cm

here. I don't be - long here.

*See top of first page of song for chord
diagram pertaining to rhythm slash.

Europa

By Carlos Santana and Tom Coster

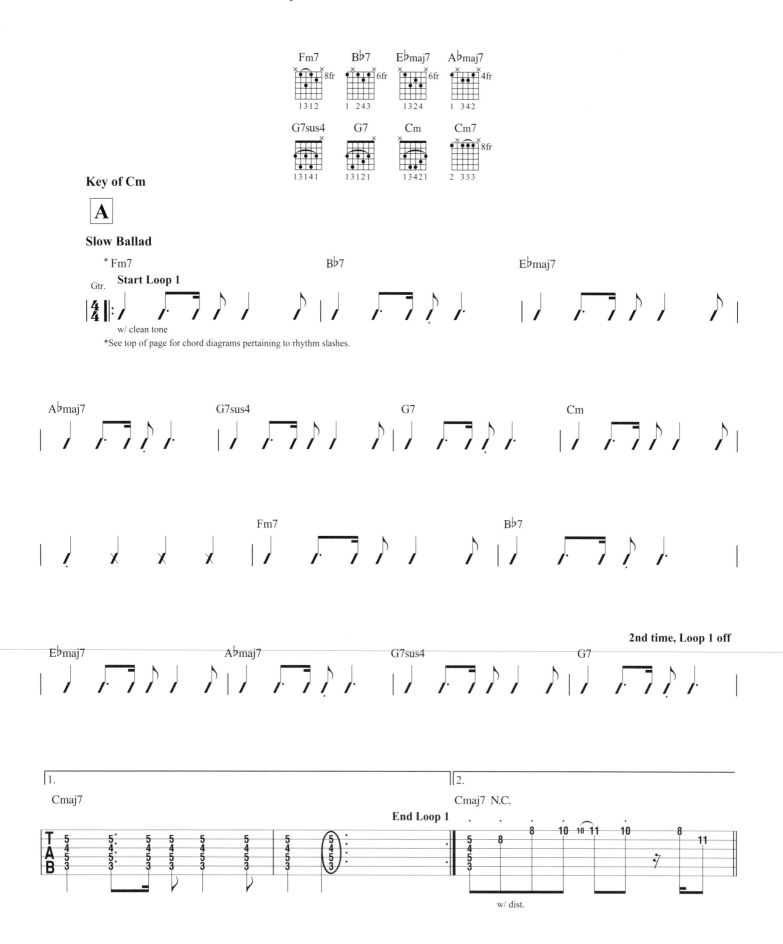

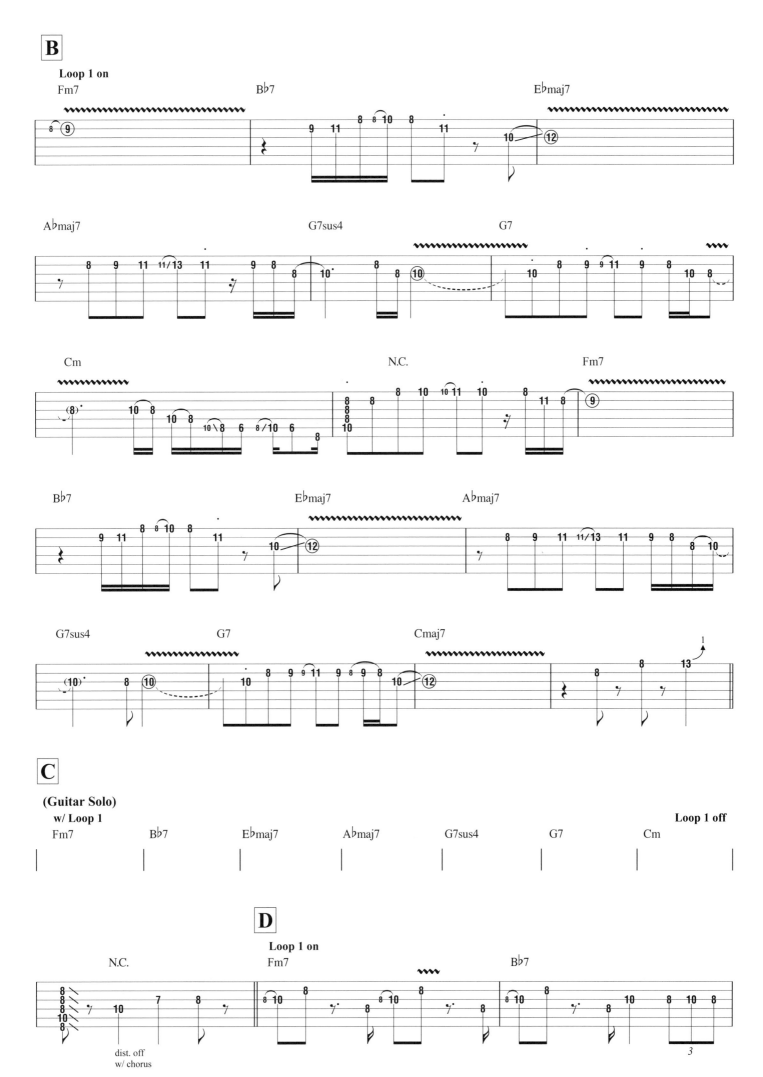

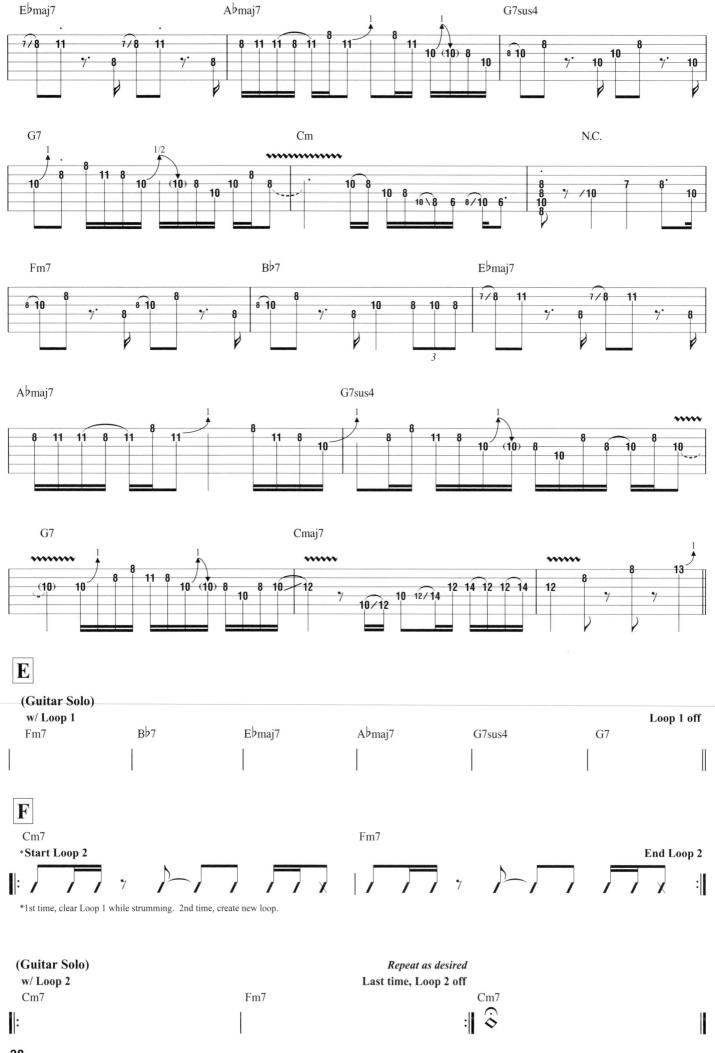

Hey Joe

Words and Music by Billy Roberts

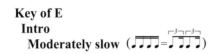

Key of E
Intro
Moderately slow

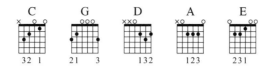

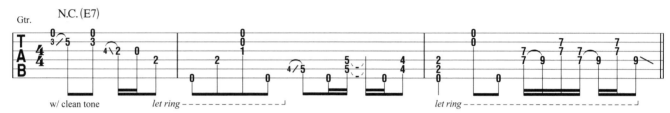

w/ clean tone   *let ring*   *let ring*

Verse

1. Hey   Joe,   uh, where you go - in' with that

C   G   D   A

Start Loop 1

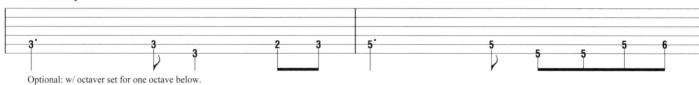

Optional: w/ octaver set for one octave below.

gun in your   hand?

E

End Loop 1

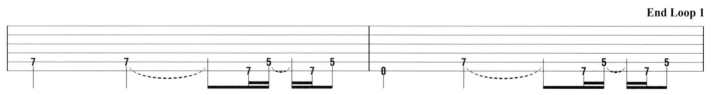

w/ Loop 1

C   G   D   A

      Hey   Joe,   I said where you go - in' with that   gun

E

in your   hand?

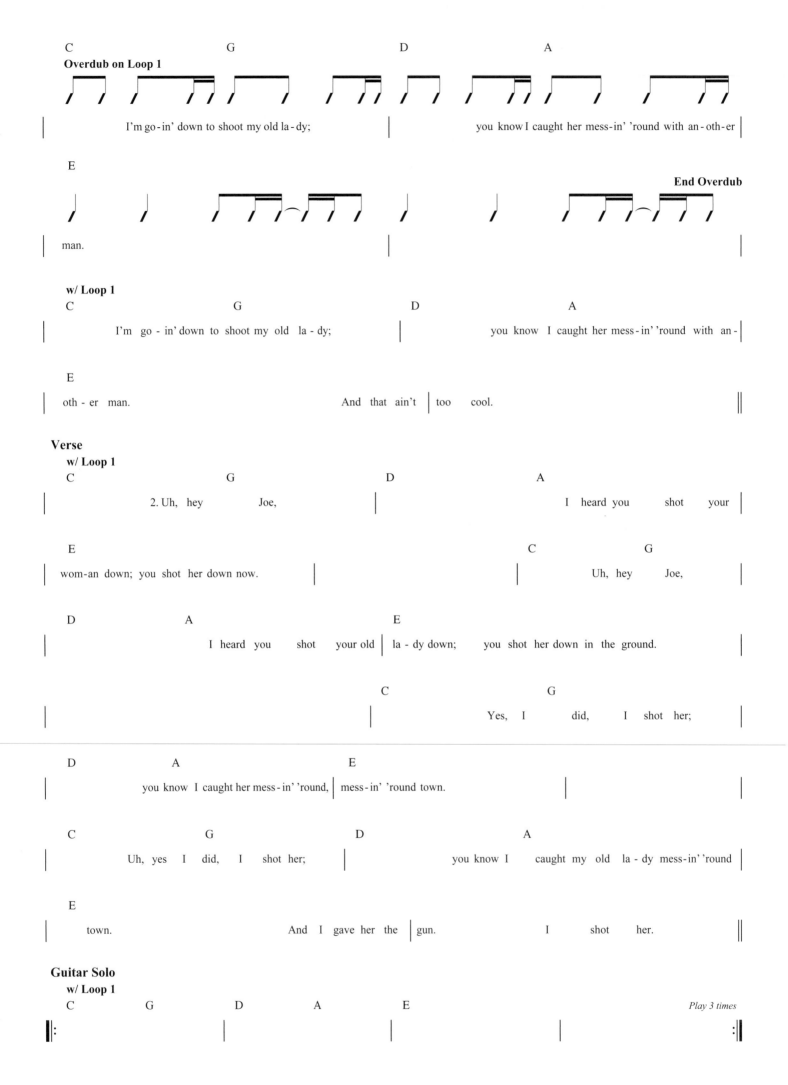

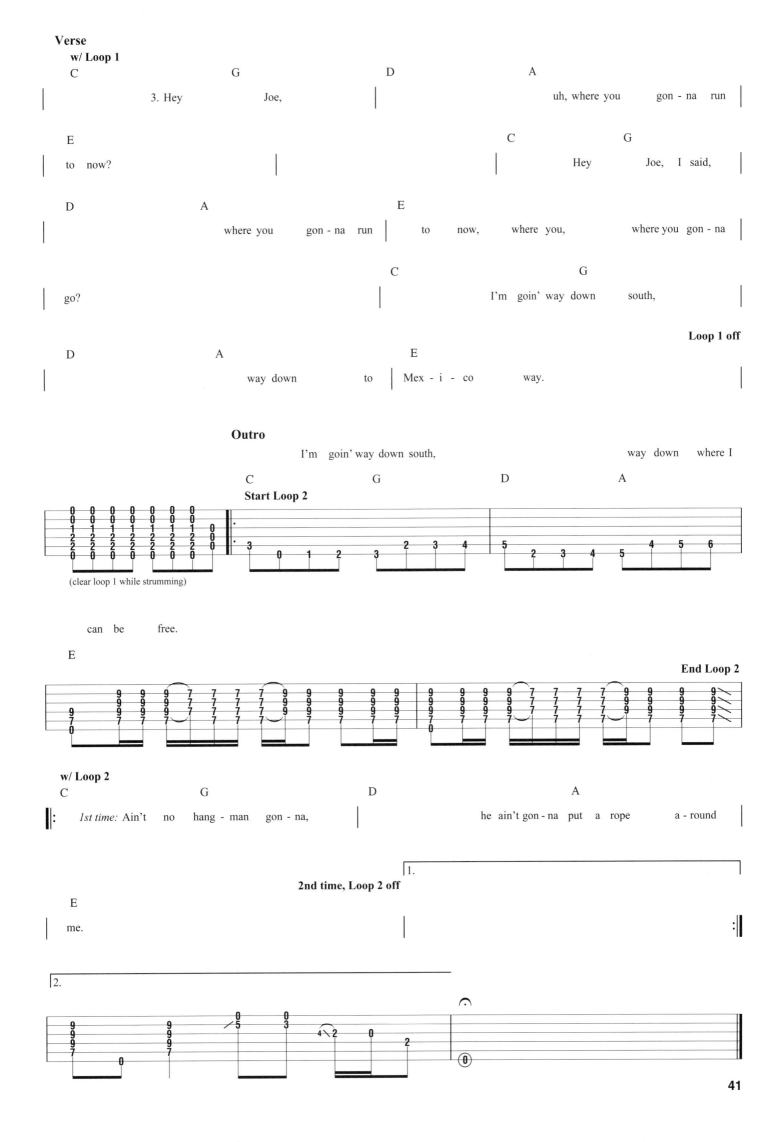

Verse

w/ Loop 1

C   G   D   A

3. Hey   Joe,   uh, where you   gon - na run

E   C   G

to   now?   Hey   Joe,   I said,

D   A   E

go?   where you   gon - na run   to   now,   where you,   where you gon - na

C   G

go?   I'm goin' way down   south,

Loop 1 off

D   A   E

way down   to   Mex - i - co   way.

Outro

I'm goin' way down south,   way down   where I

C   G   D   A

Start Loop 2

(clear loop 1 while strumming)

can   be   free.

E

End Loop 2

w/ Loop 2

C   G   D   A

1st time: Ain't   no   hang - man   gon - na,   he ain't gon - na put a rope   a - round

1.

2nd time, Loop 2 off

E

me.

2.

41

Feelin' Alright

Words and Music by Dave Mason

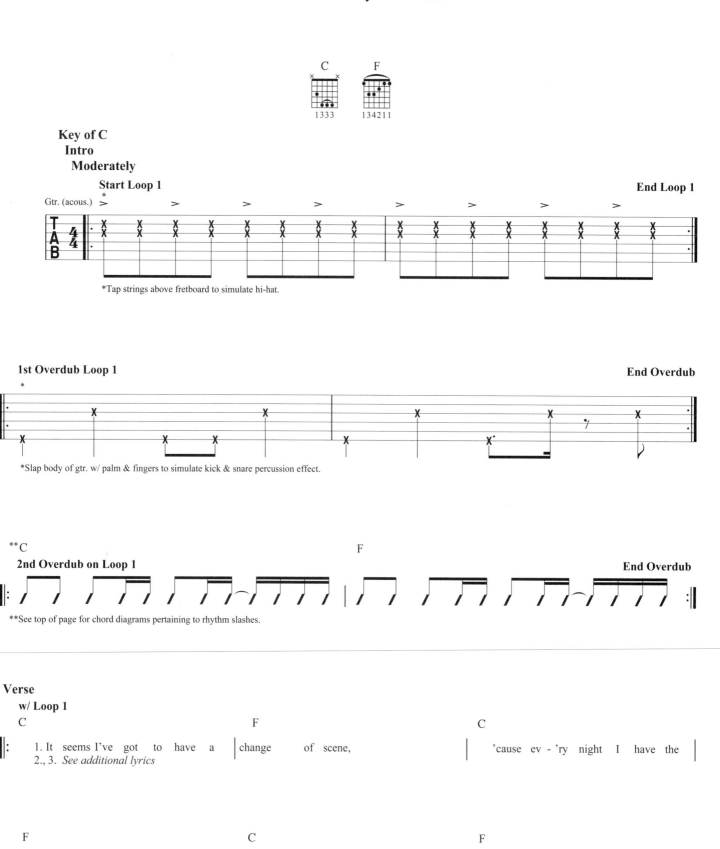

Key of C
Intro
Moderately

*Tap strings above fretboard to simulate hi-hat.

*Slap body of gtr. w/ palm & fingers to simulate kick & snare percussion effect.

**See top of page for chord diagrams pertaining to rhythm slashes.

Verse
w/ Loop 1

C	F	C
1. It seems I've got to have a	change of scene,	'cause ev - 'ry night I have the

2., 3. *See additional lyrics*

F	C	F
strang - est dream.	Pri - soned by the way it	could have been.

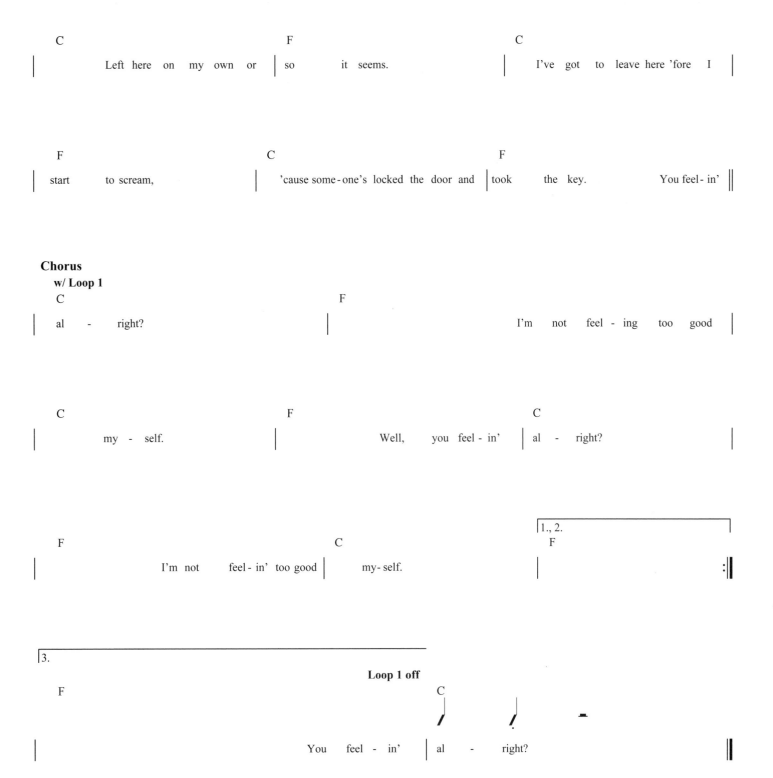

C		F		C	
Left here on my own or	so	it seems.		I've got to leave here 'fore I	

F		C		F	
start to scream,	'cause some-one's locked the door and	took the key.	You feel-in'

Chorus
w/ Loop 1

C		F			
al - right?			I'm not feel - ing too good	

C		F		C	
my - self.	Well, you feel - in'	al - right?	

1., 2.

F		C		F	
I'm not feel-in' too good	my-self.		

3.

Loop 1 off

F		C	
You feel - in'	al - right?	

Additional Lyrics

2. Well, boy, you sure took me for one big ride,
And even now I sit and wonder why.
Then when I think of you I start to cry.
I just can't waste my time; I must keep dry.
Gotta stop believin' in all your lies.
'Cause there's too much to do before I die.

3. Don't get too lost in all I say.
Though at the time I really felt that way.
But that was then and now it's today.
Can't get off yet and so I'm here to stay.
Till someone comes along and takes my place,
With a different name and, yes, a different face.

Fever

Words and Music by Dan Auerbach, Patrick Carney and Brian Burton

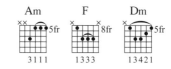

Key of Am
Intro
Moderately fast

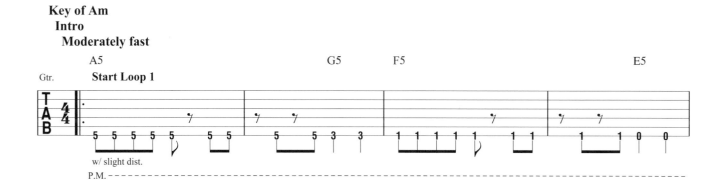

Overdub on Loop 1

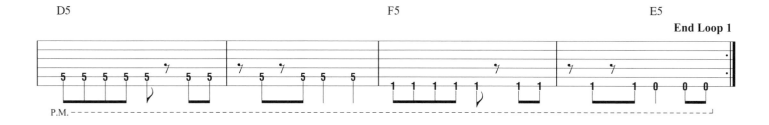

*See top of page for chord diagrams pertaining to rhythm slashes.

End Overdub

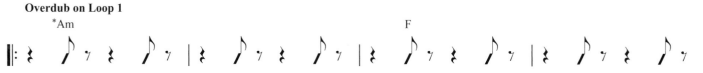

w/ Loop 1

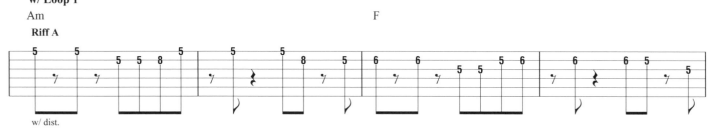

Dm   **F**

End Riff A

Verse
w/ Loop 1

A5   **G5** **F5**   **E5**
|: 1. Fe - ver, where'd you run | to? | Fe - ver, where'd you run | to? | Act - |
| 2. Fe - ver, can you hear | me? | Fe - ver, can you hear | me? | You |

D5   **F5**   **E5**
| - in' right is so rou - tine, | | and | fe - ver, let me live a dream. | | |
| shook me like I've nev - er been. | | Now | show me how to live a - gain. | Uh, |

Am   **F**
| Fe - ver, I'm a slave | to; | know I mis - be - haved | too. | Fe - |
| used to be a bless | - ing, | but | fe - ver's got me stress | - in'. | Re - |

Dm   **F**
| - ver, they mis - un - der - stood. | Would | - n't leave you if I could. | Fe - ver. ||
| - al - ize I am to blame, | but | fe - ver, let me play the game. | Fe - ver. ||

Chorus
w/ Loop 1
w/ Riff A (2 times)

Am   **F**
| Fe | - ver, 'cause I'm break - in'. | Fe | - ver, got me ach - in'. |

Dm   **F**
| Fe | - ver, why won't you ex - plain? | Break it down | a - gain. |

Am   **F**
| Fe | - ver, got me guil - ty. | Just | go a - head and kill me. |

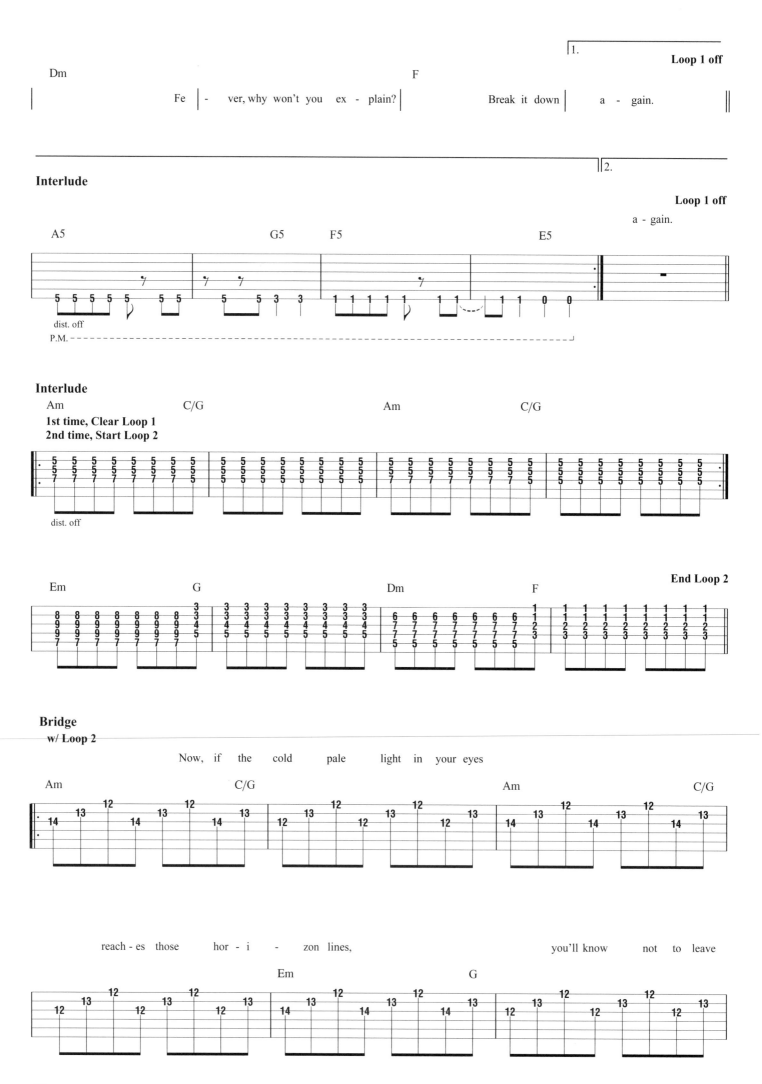

Loop 2 off

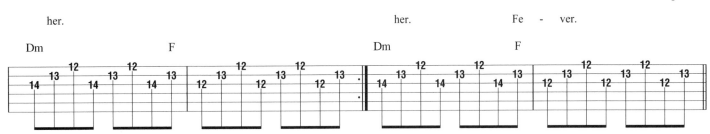

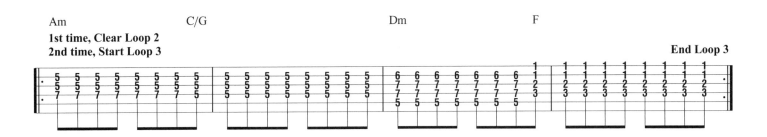

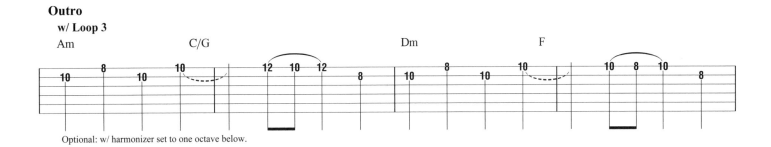

Outro

w/ Loop 3

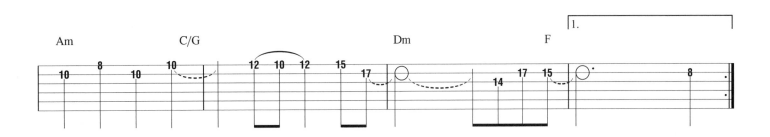

Optional: w/ harmonizer set to one octave below.

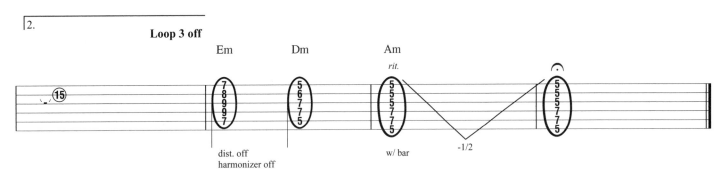

Happy

from DESPICABLE ME 2

Words and Music by Pharrell Williams

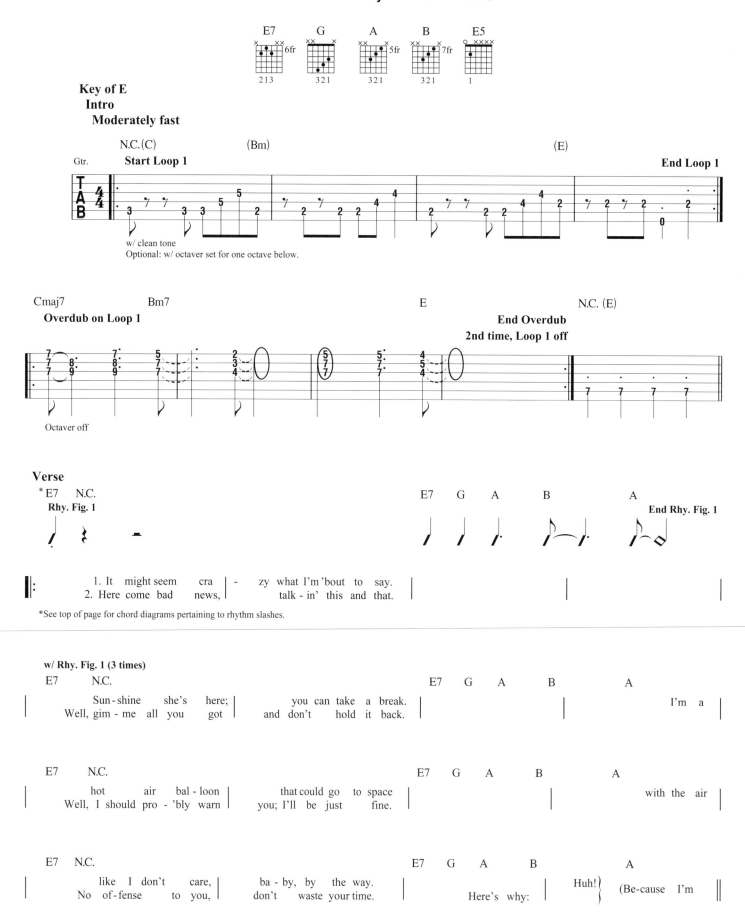

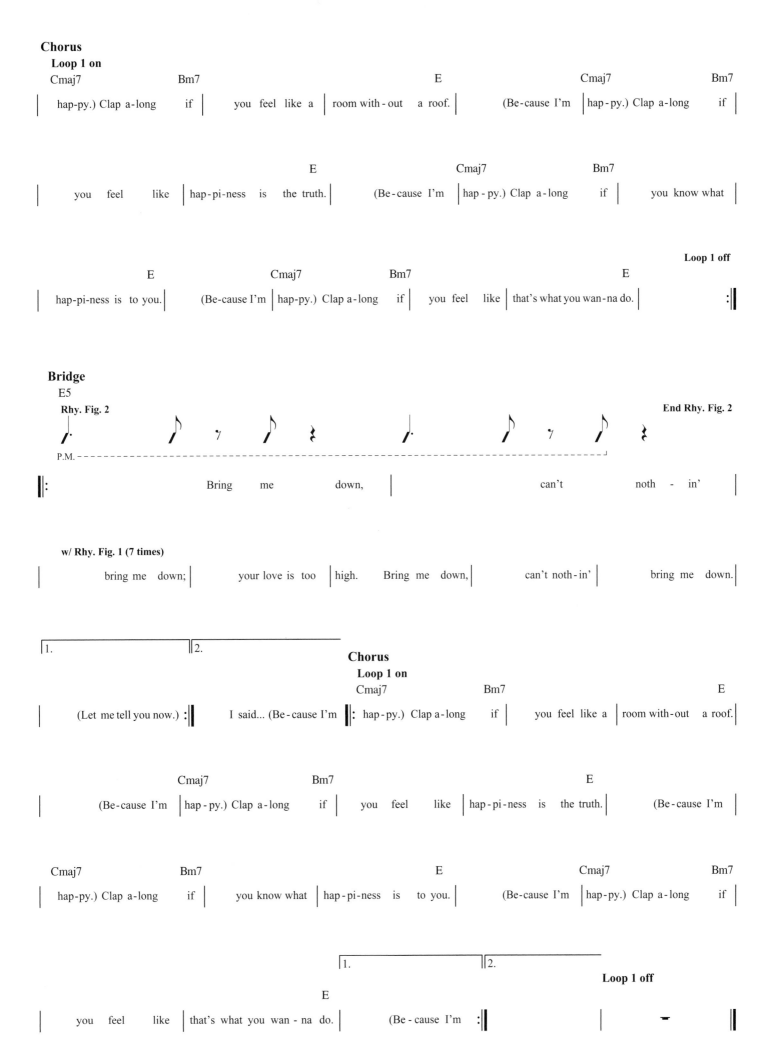

A Horse with No Name

Words and Music by Dewey Bunnell

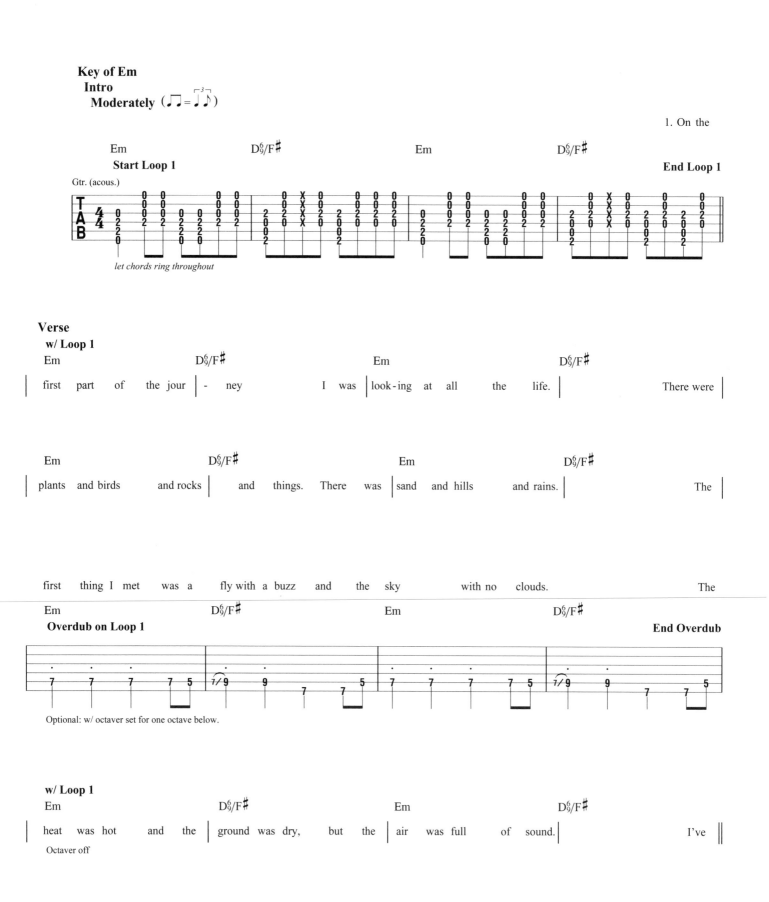

ৡ Chorus

w/ Loop 1

| Em | D$^6_9$/F# | Em | D$^6_9$/F# |

been through the des-sert on a | horse with no name. It felt | good to be out of the | rain. In the |

| Em | D$^6_9$/F# | Em | D$^6_9$/F# |

des-ert you can re- | mem-ber your name be-cause there | ain't no one for to | give you no pain. |

| Em | D$^6_9$/F# | Em | D$^6_9$/F# |

La, la, la, | la, la, la, la, la, | la, la, la. | |

To Coda ⊕

| Em | D$^6_9$/F# | Em | D$^6_9$/F# |

La, la, la, | la, la, la, la, la, | la, la, la. | 2. Af - ter ‖

Verse

w/ Loop 1

| Em | D$^6_9$/F# | Em | D$^6_9$/F# |

two days in the | des-ert sun my | skin be-gan to turn | red. Af - ter |

| Em | D$^6_9$/F# | Em | D$^6_9$/F# |

three days in the | des-ert fun I was | look-ing at a riv-er-bed. | And the |

| Em | D$^6_9$/F# | Em | D$^6_9$/F# |

sto-ry it told of a | riv-er that flowed, made me | sad to think it was | dead. You see, I've ‖

Chorus

w/ Loop 1

| Em | D$^6_9$/F# | Em | D$^6_9$/F# |

been through the des-ert on a | horse with no name. It felt | good to be out of the | rain. In the |

| Em | D$^6_9$/F# | Em | D$^6_9$/F# |

des-ert you can re- | mem-ber your name be-cause there | ain't no one for to | give you no pain. |

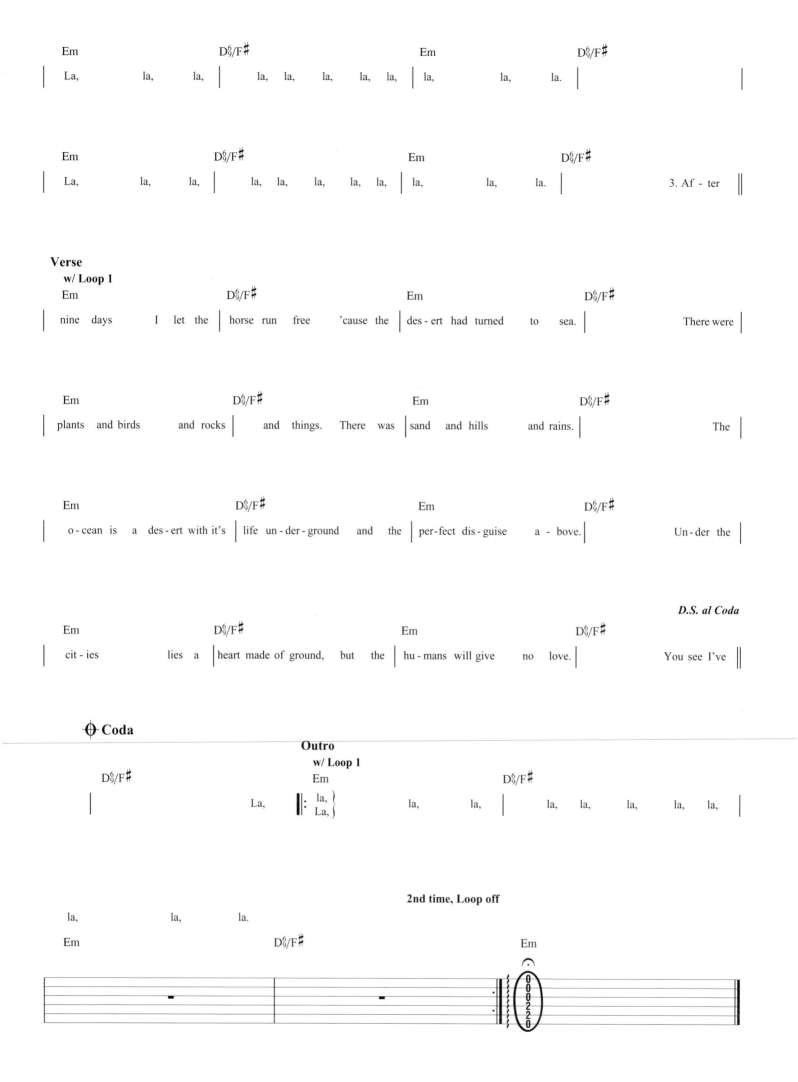

Em	D$_9^6$/F$\sharp$	Em	D$_9^6$/F$\sharp$	
La, la, la,	la, la, la, la, la,	la, la, la.		

Em	D$_9^6$/F$\sharp$	Em	D$_9^6$/F$\sharp$	
La, la, la,	la, la, la, la, la,	la, la, la.		3. Af - ter

Verse
w/ Loop 1

Em	D$_9^6$/F$\sharp$	Em	D$_9^6$/F$\sharp$	
nine days I let the	horse run free 'cause the	des - ert had turned to sea.		There were

Em	D$_9^6$/F$\sharp$	Em	D$_9^6$/F$\sharp$	
plants and birds and rocks	and things. There was	sand and hills and rains.		The

Em	D$_9^6$/F$\sharp$	Em	D$_9^6$/F$\sharp$	
o - cean is a des - ert with it's	life un - der - ground and the	per - fect dis - guise a - bove.		Un - der the

D.S. al Coda

Em	D$_9^6$/F$\sharp$	Em	D$_9^6$/F$\sharp$	
cit - ies lies a	heart made of ground, but the	hu - mans will give no love.		You see I've

Coda

Outro
w/ Loop 1

D$_9^6$/F$\sharp$	Em	D$_9^6$/F$\sharp$
La,	la, / La, \ la, la,	la, la, la, la, la,

2nd time, Loop off

la, la, la.

Em	D$_9^6$/F$\sharp$	Em

I'm Yours

Words and Music by Jason Mraz

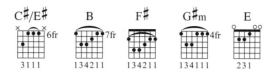

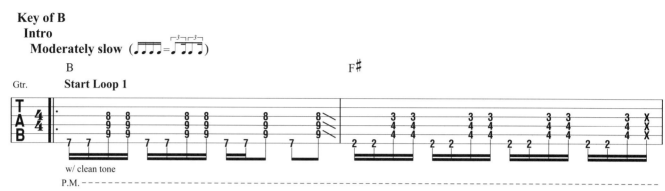

Key of B
Intro
Moderately slow

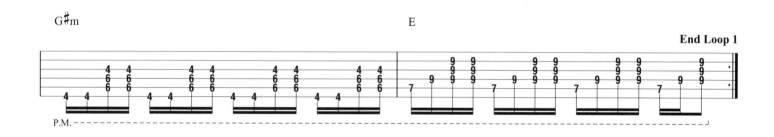

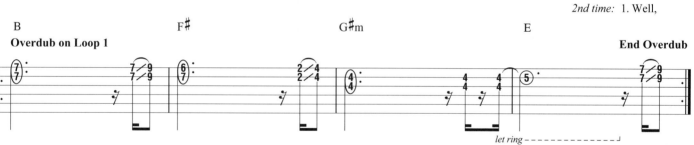

2nd time: 1. Well,

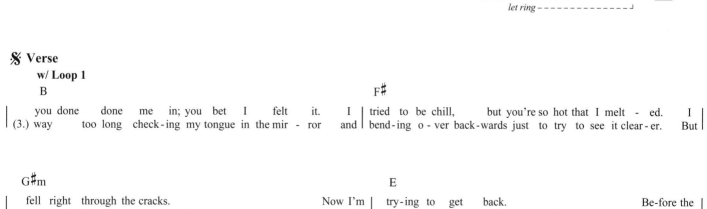

§ Verse
w/ Loop 1

B

| you done | done | me in; you bet I | felt | it. | I | tried to be chill, | but you're so hot that I melt - ed. | I |
| (3.) way | too long | check-ing my tongue in the mir - ror | and | bend-ing o - ver back-wards just to try to see it clear-er. | But |

G#m   E

| fell right through the cracks. | Now I'm | try-ing to get back. | Be-fore the |
| my breath fogged up the glass, | and so I | drew a new face and I laughed. | I |

B			F#		

cool done run out, I'll be giv-ing it my best - est, and | noth-ing's gon-na stop me but di - vine in - ter-ven - tion. I
guess what I'll be say - ing is there ain't no bet-ter rea - son to | rid your-self of van - i - ties and just go with the sea-sons. It's

To Coda ⊕

G#m			E		

reck - on it's a - gain my turn to | win some or learn some. But
what we aim to do. Our |

Chorus
w/ Loop 1

B	F#	G#m	E

I won't hes - i - | tate no more, no | more. It can - not | wait. I'm yours.

B	F#	G#m	E

Mm, | mm, hmm, mm. |

Verse
w/ Loop 1

B		F#	

2. Well, o - pen up your mind and see like me. O - pen up your plans and, damn, you're free.

G#m		E	

Look in - to your heart and you'll find | love, love, love, love.

B		F#	

Lis-ten to the mu-sic of the mo - ment; peo - ple dance and | sing. We're just one big fam - i - ly,

Loop 1 off

G#m		E	

and it's our god - for-sak - en right to be loved, loved, loved, loved,

Chorus
Loop 1 on

*C#/E#	B	F#	G#m

◇

loved. So, ‖ I won't hes - i - | tate no more, no | more. It can - not

*See top of first page of song for chord diagrams pertaining to rhythm slashes.

Loop 1 off

E	B	F#	G#m	E

wait. I'm sure. There's no | need to com-pli - | cate. Our time is | short. This is our | fate. I'm yours. ‖

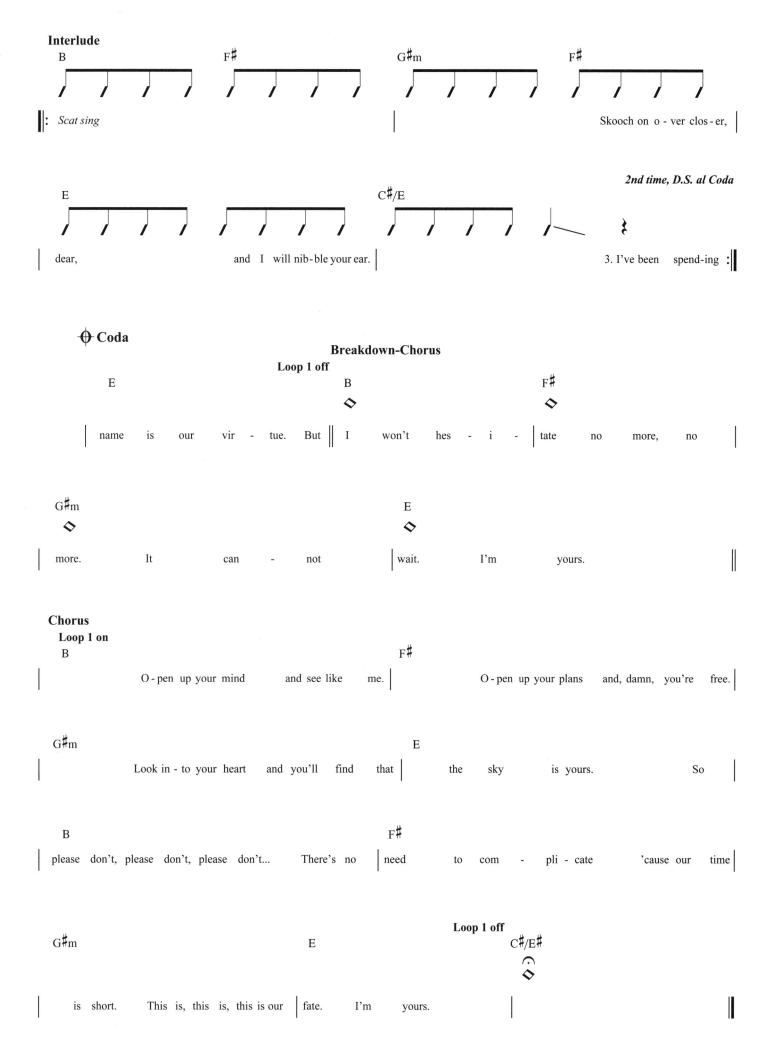

Interlude

B   F♯   G♯m   F♯

||: *Scat sing*   Skooch on o - ver clos - er,

2nd time, D.S. al Coda

E   C♯/E

dear,   and I will nib - ble your ear.   3. I've been spend-ing :||

⊕ **Coda**

Breakdown-Chorus

Loop 1 off

E   B   F♯

name is our vir - tue. But || I won't hes - i - tate no more, no

G♯m   E

more.   It can - not | wait.   I'm   yours.

Chorus

Loop 1 on

B   F♯

O - pen up your mind   and see like   me.   O - pen up your plans   and, damn, you're free.

G♯m   E

Look in - to your heart   and you'll find   that | the sky   is yours.   So

B   F♯

please don't, please don't, please don't... There's no | need   to com - pli - cate   'cause our time

Loop 1 off

G♯m   E   C♯/E♯

is short.   This is, this is, this is our | fate.   I'm   yours.

I'm Your Hoochie Coochie Man

Words and Music by Willie Dixon

Key of A
Intro
Slow Blues

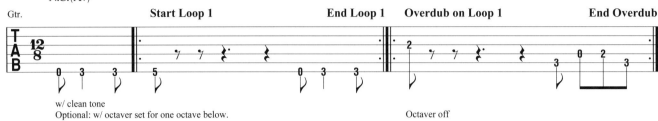

w/ clean tone
Optional: w/ octaver set for one octave below.

Octaver off

Verse
w/ Loop 1
(A7)

1. The gyp-sy wom-an told my moth-er   be-fore I was born.
2., 3. *See additional lyrics*

"You got a boy childs com-in',   gon-na be a son-of-a-gun.

Loop 1 off

He gon-na make pret-ty wom-ens   jump an' shout.   Then the world wan-na know

Chorus

what this all a-bout?"   But you know I'm here.

D7

Ev-'ry-bod-y knows I'm here.

A7

56

Well, you know I'm the Hoo - chie Coo-chie Man.

Ev - 'ry-bod - y knows I'm here.

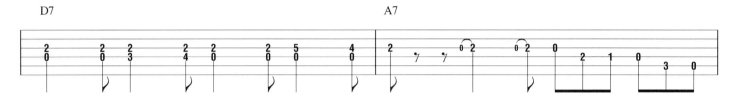

1.
2.
D.S. al Coda

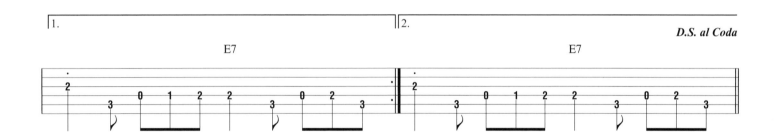

⊕ **Coda**

the whole round world knows I'm here.

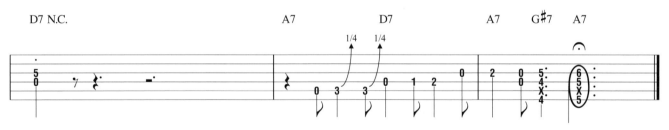

Additional Lyrics

2. I got a black cat bone,
I got a mojo too.
I got the John the Conquerroot,
I'm gonna mess with you.
I'm gonna make you girls
Lead me by the hand.
Then the world'll know
I'm the Hoochie Coochie man.

3. On the seventh hour,
On the seventh day,
On the seventh month,
The seventh doctor say,
"You were born for good luck,
And that you'll see."
I got seven hundred dollars,
Don't you mess with me.

The Joker

Words and Music by Steve Miller, Eddie Curtis and Ahmet Ertegun

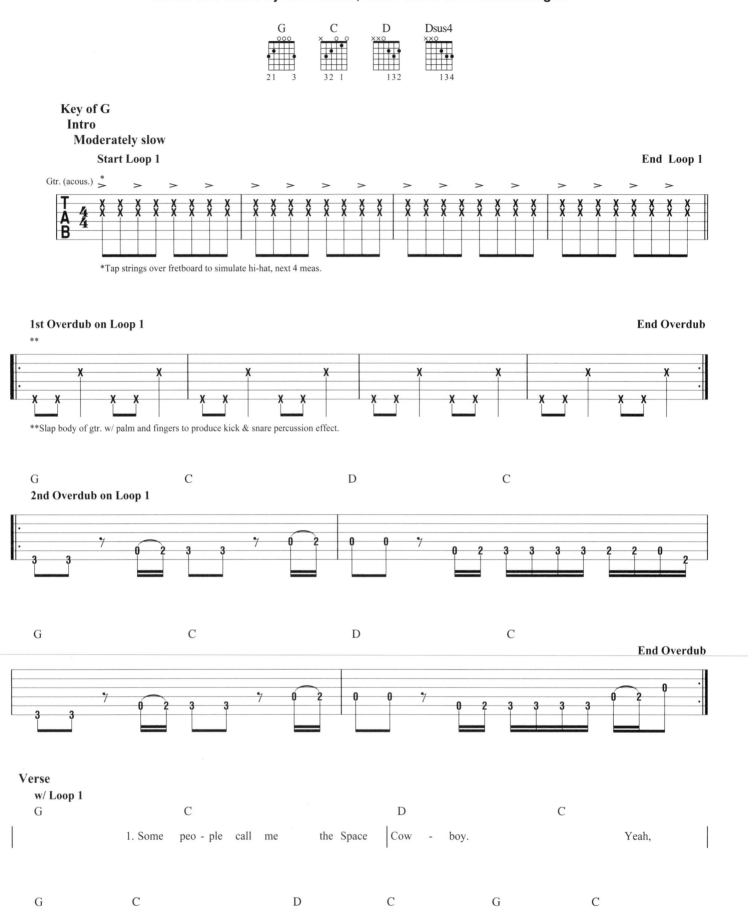

*Tap strings over fretboard to simulate hi-hat, next 4 meas.

**Slap body of gtr. w/ palm and fingers to produce kick & snare percussion effect.

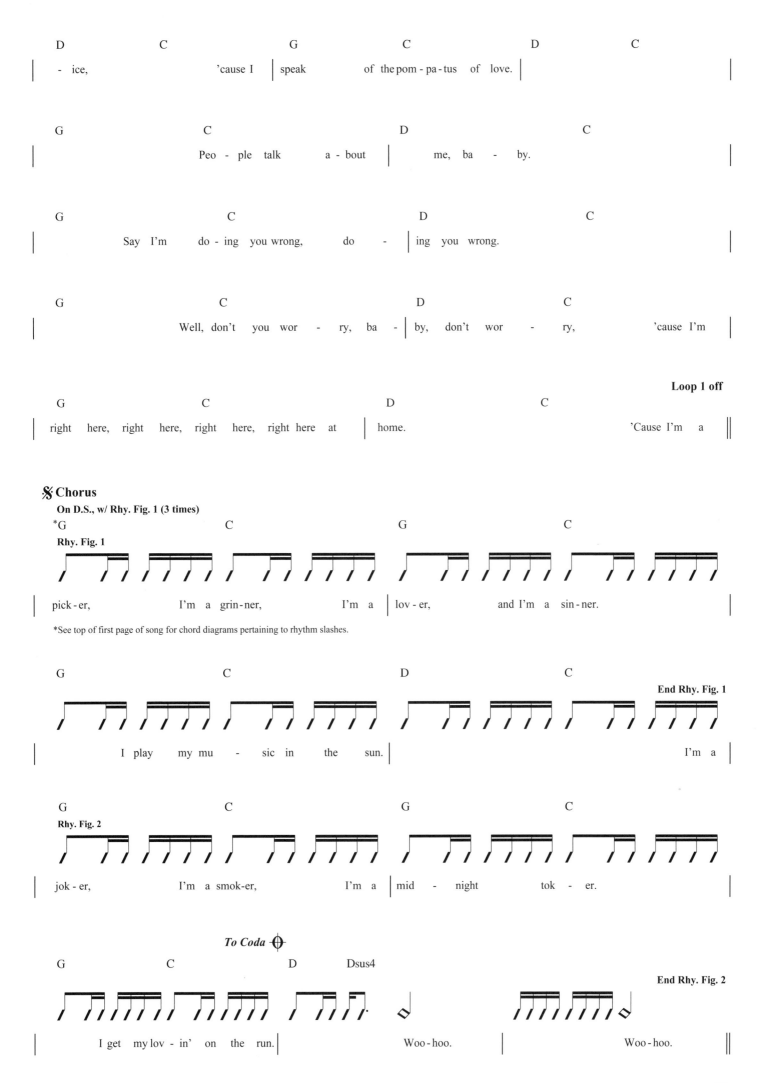

Guitar Solo

Loop 1 on

| G | C | D | C | G | C | D | C |

Verse

w/ Loop 1

G   C   D   C

2. You're the cut - est thing that I ev | - er did see.   I

G   C   D   C

real - ly love your peach - es, want to | shake your tree.

G   C   D   C

Love - y dove - y, love - y dove - y, love - y | dove - y all the time.

D.S. al Coda

Loop 1 off

G   C   D   C

Oo, wee, ba - by, I'll sure show | you a good time.   'Cause I'm a

Coda

D   C   G   C

           I'm a | pick - er,   I'm a grin - ner,   I'm a

G   C   G   C

lov - er, and I'm a sin - ner. | I play my mu - sic in the sun.

w/ Rhy. Fig. 2

D   C   G   C

           I'm a | jok - er,   I'm a smok - er,   I'm a

G   C   G   C

mid - night tok - er. | I sure don't want to hurt no

D   Dsus4   G

one.   Woo - hoo. | Woo - hoo.

Nutshell

Words by Layne Staley
Music by Jerry Cantrell, Mike Inez and Sean Kinney

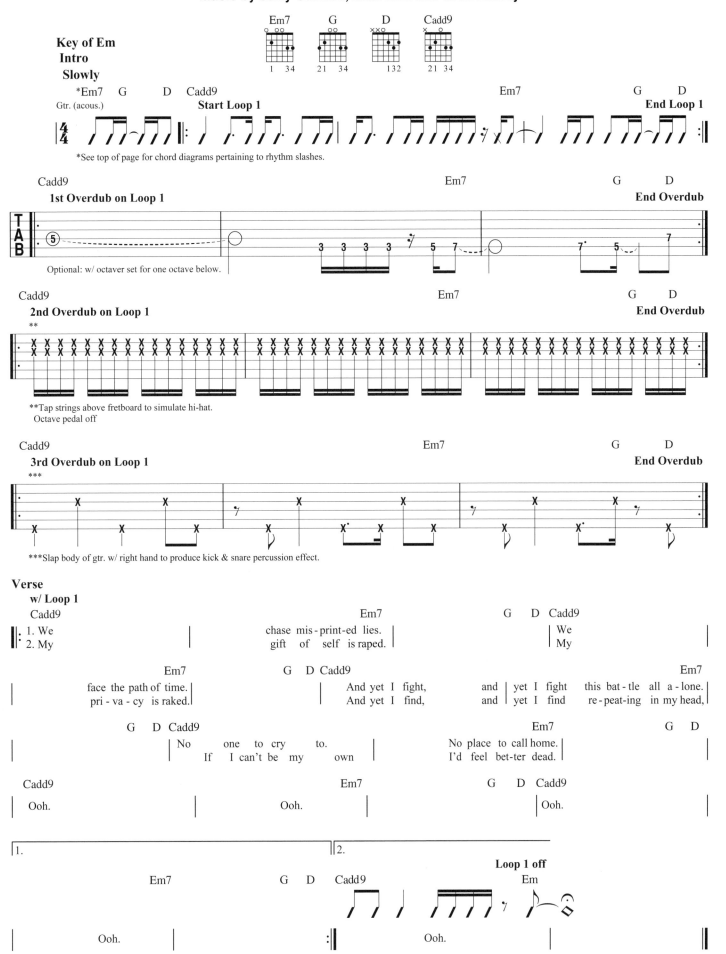

Knockin' on Heaven's Door

Words and Music by Bob Dylan

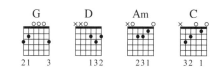

Key of G
Intro
Slowly

Start Loop 1   **End Loop 1**

Gtr. (acous.)

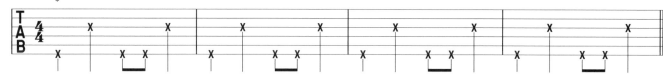

*Slap body of gtr. w/ palm and fingers to produce kick & snare percussion effect, next 4 meas.

Overdub on Loop 1   **End Overdub**

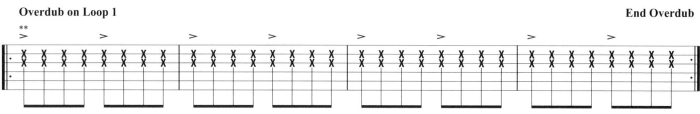

**Tap strings over fretboard to simulate hi-hat, next 4 meas.

***G   D   Am

2nd Overdub on Loop 1

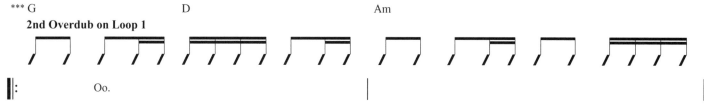

Oo.

***See top of page for chord diagrams pertaining to rhythm slashes.

G   D   C

Oo.   **End Overdub**

𝄋 **Verse**

w/ Loop 1
G   D   Am   G   D

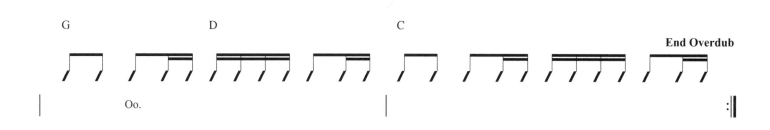

1. Ma - ma, take this badge off   of   me.   I can't use   it   an - y - more.
2. See additional lyrics

C   G   D

| It's get-tin' dark,   too dark for me to see. |

Am   G   D   C

| I feel I'm knock-in' on heav-en's door. ‖

Chorus
w/ Loop 1
G   D   Am

‖: Knock, knock knock-in' on heav-en's door. |

                                                    ⌐1.   ⌐2.
              4th time, To Coda ⊕   *D.S. al Coda*
                                                                                     (take repeat)
G   D   C   C

| Knock, knock, knock-in' on heav-en's door. | :‖   ‖

⊕ **Coda**

                              Outro
                              w/ Loop 1
              C   G   D   Am

              | ‖:   Oo. | |

                              2nd time, Loop 1 off
G   D   C   G

| Oo. | :‖   ‖

Additional Lyrics

2. Mama, put my guns in the ground.
   I can't shoot them anymore.
   That long black cloud is comin' down.
   I feel I'm knockin' on heaven's door.

63

Learning to Fly

Words and Music by Tom Petty and Jeff Lynne

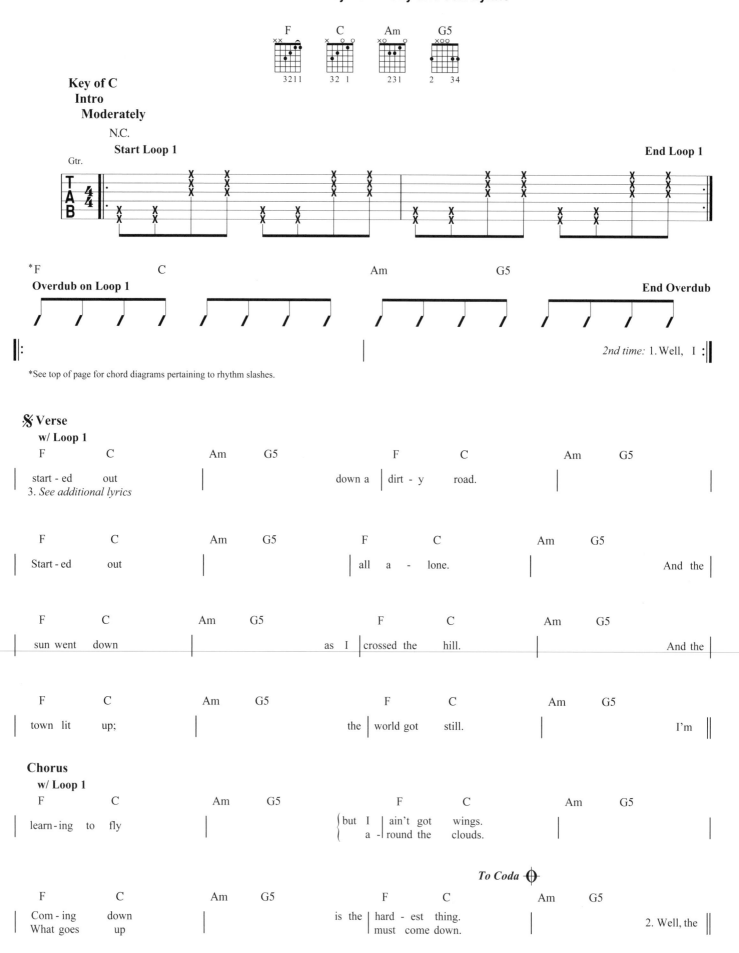

Key of C
Intro
Moderately

*See top of page for chord diagrams pertaining to rhythm slashes.

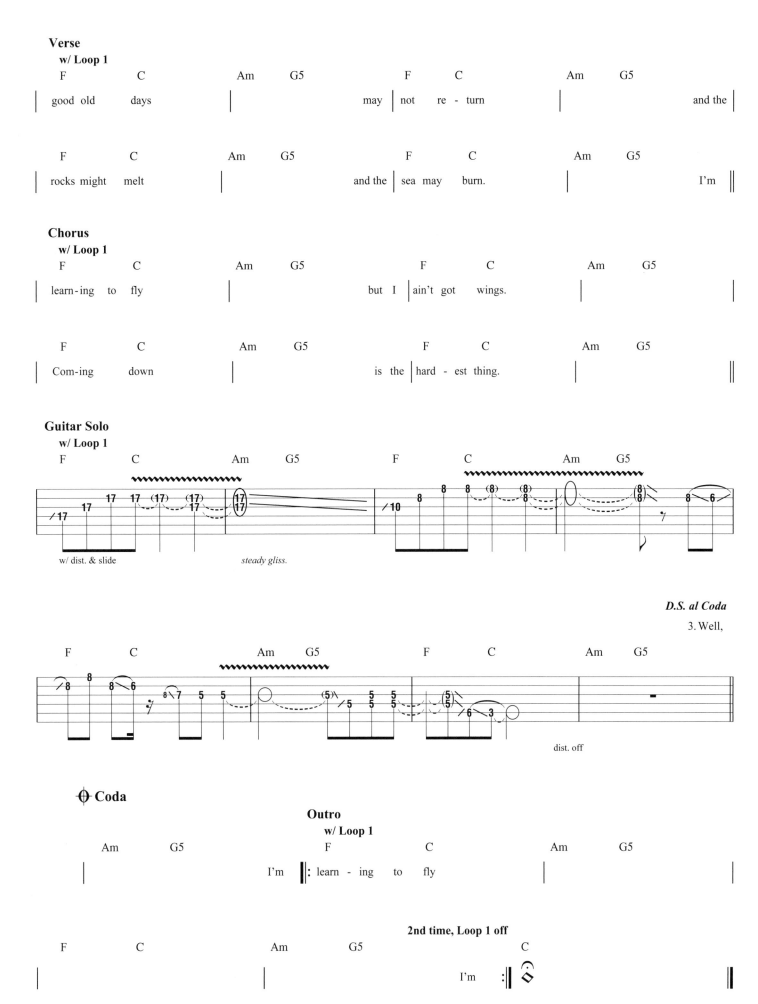

Verse

w/ Loop 1

F	C		Am	G5		F	C		Am	G5	

good old days | may not re - turn | and the |

| F | C | | Am | G5 | | F | C | | Am | G5 | |

rocks might melt | and the sea may burn. | I'm ‖

Chorus

w/ Loop 1

| F | C | | Am | G5 | | F | C | | Am | G5 | |

learn-ing to fly | but I ain't got wings. |

| F | C | | Am | G5 | | F | C | | Am | G5 | |

Com-ing down | is the hard - est thing. ‖

Guitar Solo

w/ Loop 1

| F | C | | Am | G5 | | F | C | | Am | G5 | |

w/ dist. & slide   *steady gliss.*

D.S. al Coda

3. Well,

| F | C | | Am | G5 | | F | C | | Am | G5 | |

dist. off

⊕ Coda

Outro

w/ Loop 1

| Am | G5 | | F | C | | Am | G5 | |

I'm ‖: learn - ing to fly |

2nd time, Loop 1 off

| F | C | | Am | G5 | | C | |

I'm :‖

Additional Lyrics

3. Well, some say life will beat you down,
   And break your heart, steal your crown.
   So I've started out for God knows where.
   I guess I'll know when I get there.

65

Radioactive

Words and Music by Daniel Reynolds, Benjamin McKee, Daniel Sermon, Alexander Grant and Josh Mosser

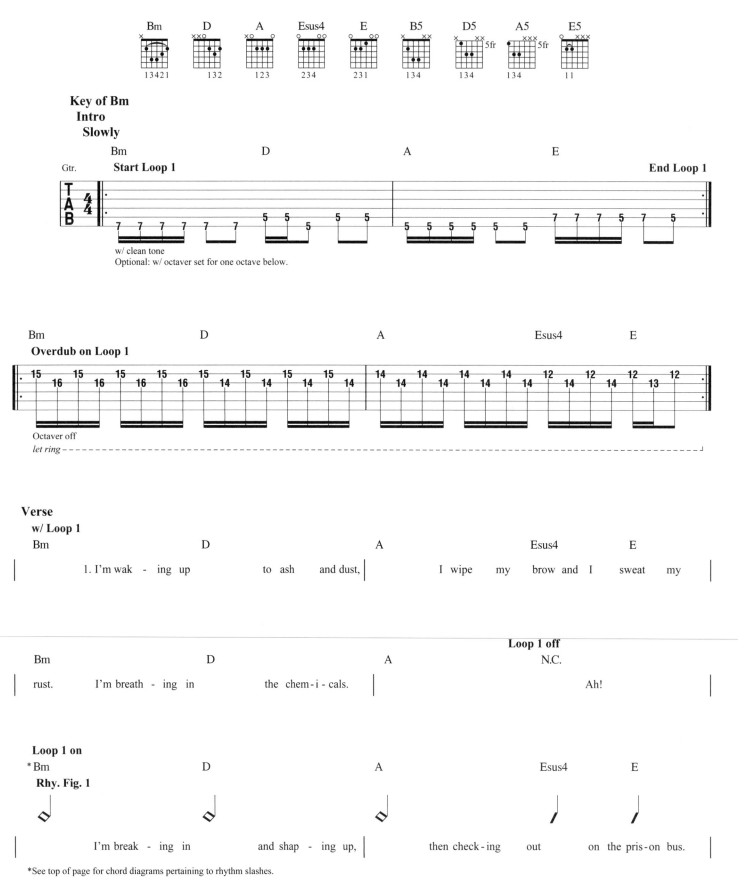

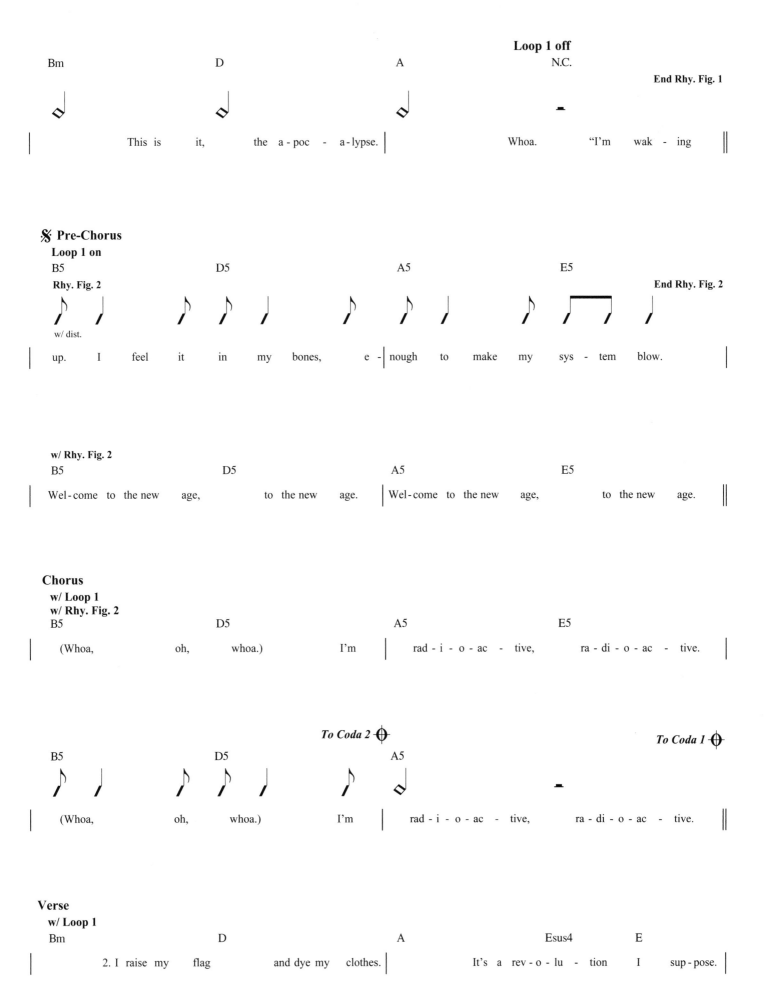

Bm	D	A	Esus4	E

We're paint - ed red to fit right in, whoa.

w/ Rhy. Fig. 1

Bm	D	A	Esus4	E

I'm break - ing in and shap - ing up, then check - ing out on the pris - on bus.

D.S. al Coda 1

Loop 1 off

Bm	D	A	N.C.

This is it, the a - poc - a - lypse. Whoa. I'm wak - ing

⊕ Coda 1

Bridge

Loop 1 off

All sys - tems go, the sun has - n't died.

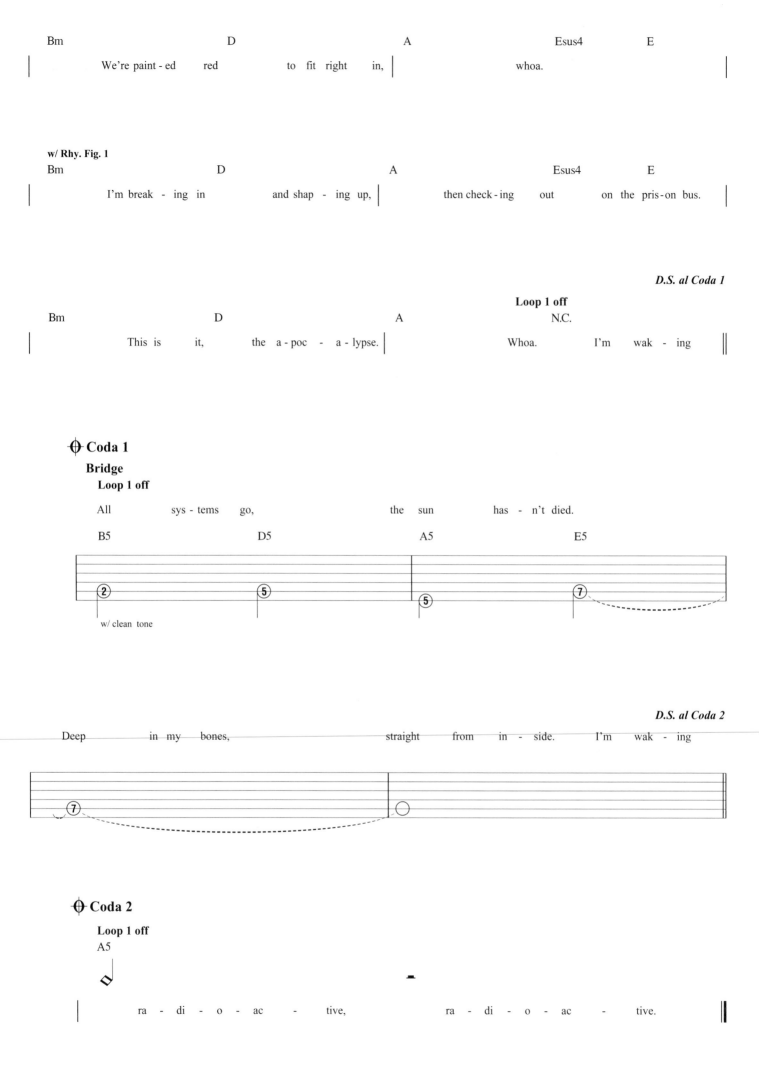

B5   D5   A5   E5

w/ clean tone

D.S. al Coda 2

Deep in my bones, straight from in - side. I'm wak - ing

⊕ Coda 2

Loop 1 off

A5

ra - di - o - ac - tive, ra - di - o - ac - tive.

Round Here

Words and Music by Adam Duritz, David Bryson, Charles Gillingham, Matthew Malley, Steve Bowman, Christopher Roldan, David Janusko and Dan Jewett

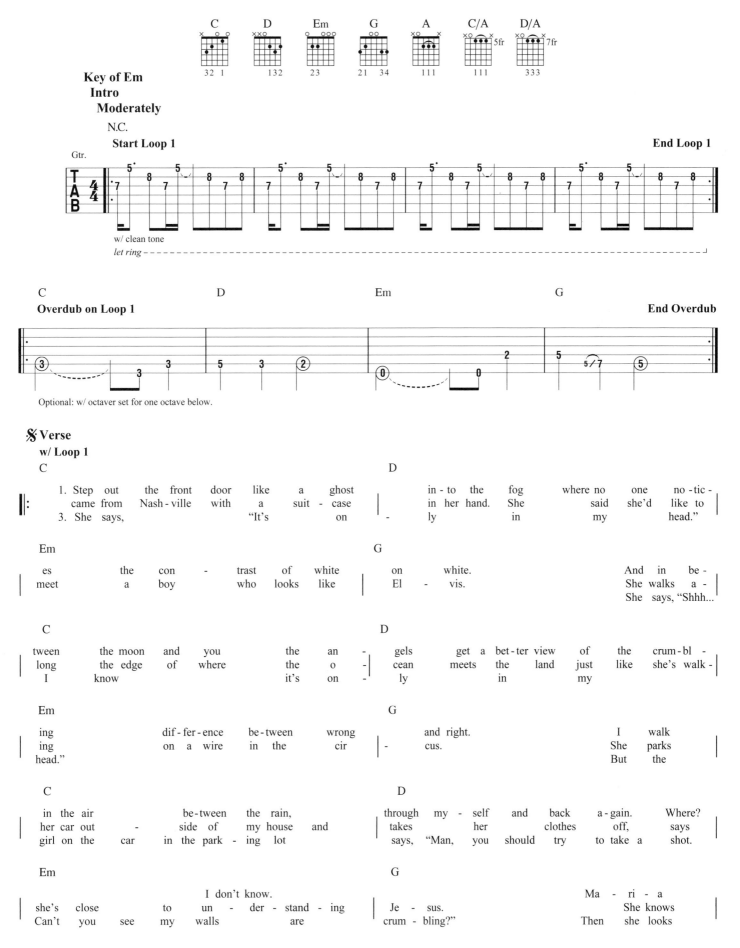

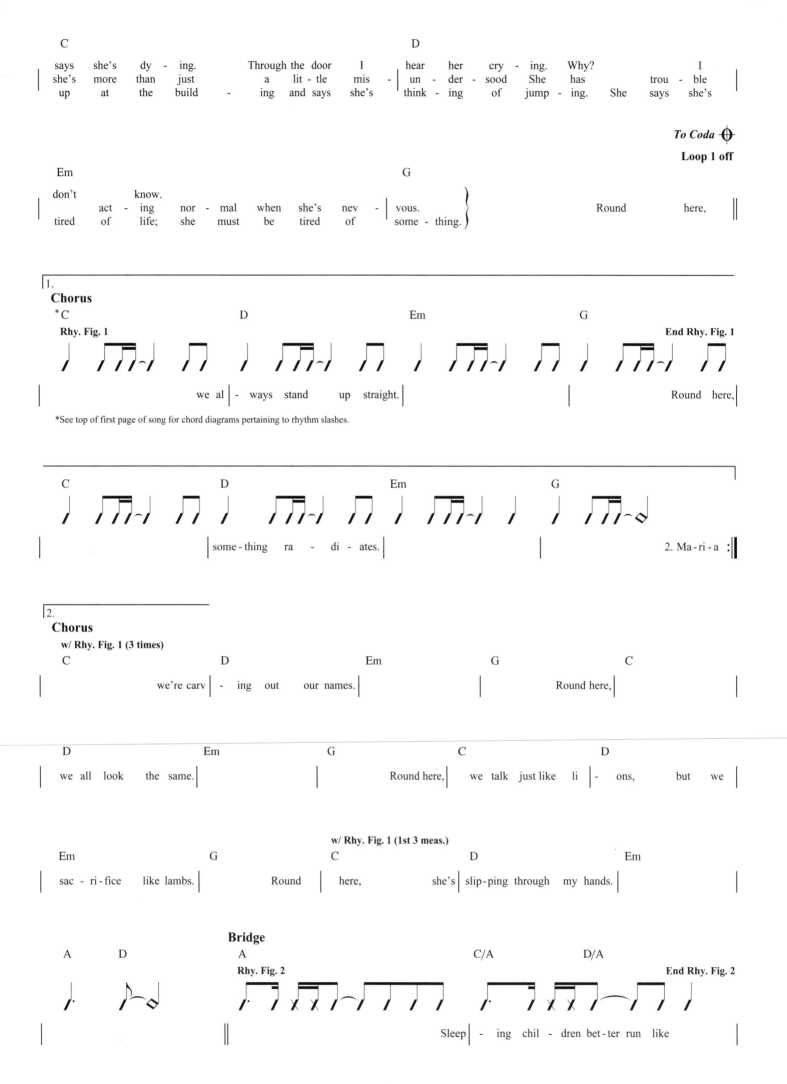

C / **D**

says | she's | dy - | ing. | | Through the door | I | | hear | her | cry - | ing. | Why? | | | I
she's | more | than | just | | a | lit - tle | mis - | | un - | der - | sood | She | has | | trou - | ble
up | at | the | build | - | ing | and says | she's | | think - | ing | of | jump - | ing. | | She | says | she's

To Coda ✛

Loop 1 off

Em / **G**

don't | | know. | | | | | |
| act - | ing | nor - | mal | when | she's | nev - | vous. | } | | Round | | here,
tired | of | life; | she | must | be | tired | of | | some - | thing. | | |

1.

Chorus

C / D / Em / G

Rhy. Fig. 1   **End Rhy. Fig. 1**

we al | - ways stand | up straight. | | | Round here,

*See top of first page of song for chord diagrams pertaining to rhythm slashes.

C / D / Em / G

some - thing ra - | di - ates. | | | 2. Ma - ri - a :‖

2.

Chorus

w/ Rhy. Fig. 1 (3 times)

C / D / Em / G / C

we're carv | - ing out our names. | | Round here, | |

D / Em / G / C / D

we all look the same. | | Round here, | we talk just like li | - ons, but we

w/ Rhy. Fig. 1 (1st 3 meas.)

Em / G / C / D / Em

sac - ri - fice like lambs. | Round | here, | she's | slip - ping through my hands. | |

Bridge

A / D / A / C/A / D/A

Rhy. Fig. 2   **End Rhy. Fig. 2**

Sleep | - ing chil - dren bet - ter run like

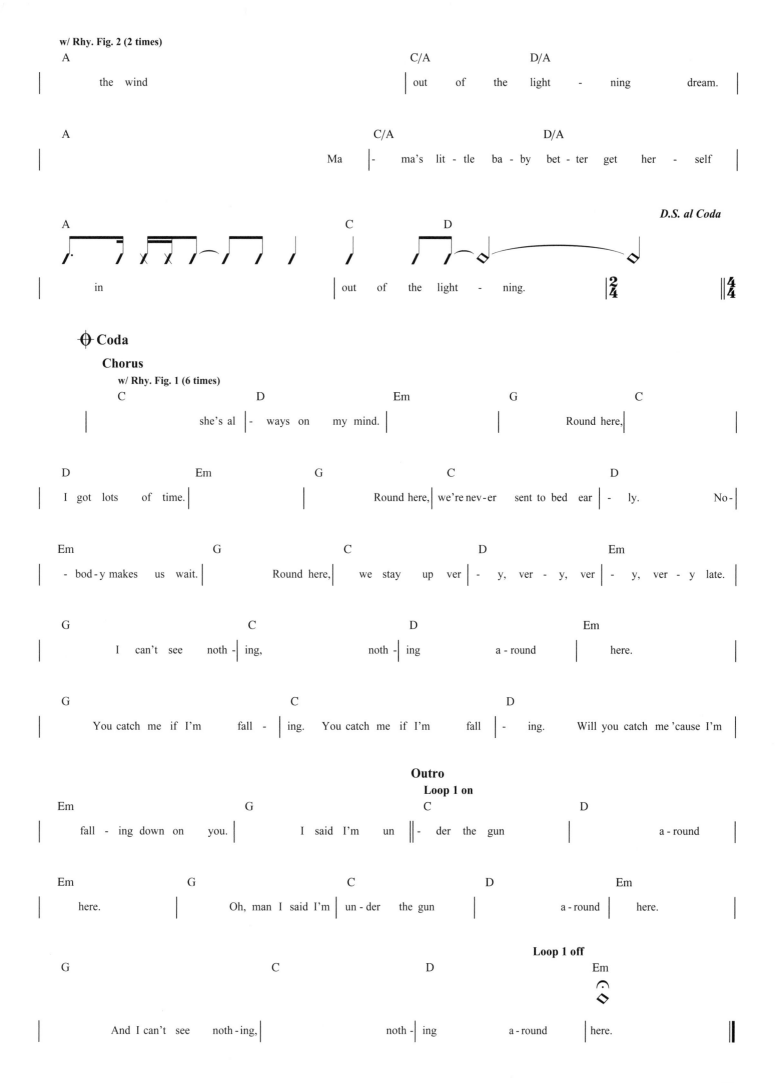

Run-Around

Words and Music by John Popper

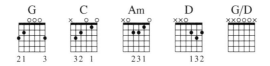

Key of G
Intro
Moderately

Start Loop 1   **End Loop 1**

Gtr. (acous.)   *

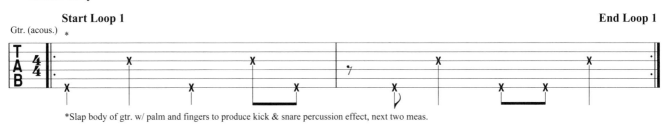

*Slap body of gtr. w/ palm and fingers to produce kick & snare percussion effect, next two meas.

**G   C   Am   D   G/D

Overdub on Loop 1   **End Overdub**

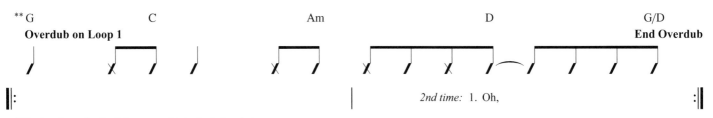

2nd time: 1. Oh,

**See top of page for chord diagrams pertaining to rhythm slashes.

Verse
w/ Loop 1

| G | C | Am | D | G/D | G | C | Am | D | G/D |

once up - on   a mid - night drear - y I woke   with some-thing in my   head.   I
2. *See additional lyrics*

| G | C | Am | D | G/D | G | C | Am | D | G/D |

could-n't es-cape   the mem - o - ry   of a phone   call and of   what you   said.   Like a

| G | C | Am | D | G/D | G | C | Am | D | G/D |

game show con-tes-tant with a part - ing   gift,   I could not   be - lieve   my eyes   when I saw

| G | C | Am | D | G/D | G | C | Am | D | G/D |

through the voice   of a trust - ed   friend who needs to   hu-mor me and   tell   me   lies.   Yeah, hu -

| G | C | Am | D | G/D | G | C | Am | D | G/D |

\- mor me and tell me │ lies. And │ I'll lie too and say I │ don't mind, and │

| G | C | Am | D | G/D | G | C | Am | D | G/D |

as we seek, so shall │ we find. And │ when you're feel-ing o - pen I'll still │ be here, but │

| G | C | Am | D | G/D | G | C | Am | D | G/D |

not with-out a cer-tain de-gree │ of fear of │ what will be with │ you and me. I still │

Chorus
w/ Loop 1

| G | C | Am | D | G/D | G | C | Am | D | G/D |

can see things hope │- ful - ly. But you, ‖ │ why you wan - na │

| G | C | Am | D | G/D | G | C | Am | D | G/D |

give me a run - a - round? │ Is it a sure │- fire way to speed │ things up? When │

| G | C | Am | D | G/D | G | C | Am | D | G/D |

all it does is slow │ me │ down. │ :‖

Solo
w/ Loop 1

11

Verse
w/ Loop 1

| | | D | G/D | G | C | Am | D | G/D |

3. Tra, la, la, bom ‖- ba, dear, this is │ the pi - lot speak-ing, and I've │

| G | C | Am | D | G/D | G | C | Am | D | G/D |

got some news for you. │ It seems my │ ship still stands no mat-ter │ what you drop, and there ain't a │

| G | C | Am | D | G/D | G | C | Am | D | G/D |

whole lot that you can do. │ Oh, sure, the │ ban-ner may be torn and the wind's │ got-ten cold - er, │

| G | C | Am | D | G/D | G | C | Am | D | G/D |

per-haps I've grown a lit-tle cyn-i -│ cal, but I │ know no mat-ter what the wait │- ress brings I shall drink│

| G | C | Am | D | G/D | G | C | Am | D | G/D |

in and al-ways be | full. Yeah, I will | drink it and al-ways be | full. Oh, |

| G | C | Am | D | G/D | G | C | Am | D | G/D |

I like cof-fee and I | like tea, but to | be a-ble to en-ter a fi | - nal plea. I |

| G | C | Am | D | G/D | G | C | Am | D | G/D |

still got this dream that you just | can't shake. I | love you to the point you can no | long-er take. Well, al-right, |

| G | C | Am | D | G/D | G | C | Am | D | G/D |

o - kay, so | be that way. I | hope and pray that there's some - | thing left to say, But ‖

Chorus
w/ Loop 1

| G | C | Am | D | G/D | G | C | Am | D | G/D |

you, | why you wan-na | give me a run - a - round? Is it a sure - |

| G | C | Am | D | G/D | G | C | Am | D | G/D |

- fire way to speed | things up? When | all it does is slow me | down. Oh, |

| G | C | Am | D | G/D | G | C | Am | D | G/D |

you, | why you wan-na | give me a run-a - round? Is it a sure |

Loop 1 off

| G | C | Am | D | G/D | G | C | Am | D | G/D G |

fire way to speed | things up? When | all it does is slow | me | down. ‖

Additional Lyrics

2. And shake me and my confidence
About a great many things.
But I've been there, I can see it cower
Like a nervous magician waiting in the wings
Of a bad play where the heroes are right
And nobody thinks or expects too much.
And Hollywood's calling for the movie rights,
Singing, "Hey babe, let's keep in touch.
Hey baby, let's keep in touch."
But I want more than a touch, I want you to reach me
And show me all the things no one else can see.
So what you feel becomes mine as well.
And soon, if we're lucky, we'd be unable to tell
What's yours and mine, the fishing's fine,
And it doesn't have to rhyme, so don't you feed me a line.

Shape of You

Words and Music by Ed Sheeran, Kevin Briggs, Kandi Burruss, Tameka Cottle, Steve Mac and Johnny McDaid

Key of Bm
Intro
Moderately slow

Start Loop 1

End Loop 1

Gtr. (acous.) *

*Slap body of gtr. w/ right hand palm and fingers to produce kick & snare percussion effect.

N.C.(Bm)   (Em)   (G)   (A)

1st Overdub on Loop 1

End Overdub

P.M. -

2nd time: 1. The

Bm   Em   G   A

2nd Overdub on Loop 1

End Overdub

P.M. -

Verse
w/ Loop 1

Bm   Em   G   A

club is - n't the best place   to find a lov - er, so the | bar is where I   go.

you. 2. *See additional lyrics*

Bm   Em   G   A

Me and my friends   at   the ta - ble do - ing shots, drink - ing | fast, and then we talk   slow.   And you come

Bm   Em   G   A

o - ver and start up a con - ver - sa - tion with just   me   and, | trust me, I'll give it   a chance.   Now, take my

Bm			Em		G		A	

hand, stop, put Van the Man on the juke - box, and │ then we start to dance, and now I'm sing - ing like,

Pre-Chorus

Bm	Em	G	A

"Girl, you know I want your love. │ Your love was hand - made for some - bod - y like

Bm	Em	G	A

me. Come on, now, fol - low my lead. │ I may be cra - zy, don't mind me. Say,

Bm	Em	G	A

'Boy, let's not talk too much. │ Grab on my waist and put that bod - y on

Loop 1 off

Bm	Em	G	N.C.

me.' Come on, now, fol - low my lead. Come, │ come on, now, fol - low my lead." Mm.

𝄋 Chorus

Loop 1 on

Bm	Em	G	A

I'm in love with the shape of │ you. We push and pull like a mag - net

Bm	Em	G	A

do. Al - though my heart is fall - ing, │ too, I'm in love with your bod - y.

Bm	Em	G	A

Last night you were in my │ room, and now my bed sheets smell like

3rd time, To Coda ⊕

Bm	Em	G	A

you. Ev - 'ry day dis - cov - er - ing some - thing brand │ new. Well, I'm in love with your bod - y.

Bm	Em	G	A

Oh, I, oh, I, oh, I, oh, I. │ Well, I'm in love with your bod - y.

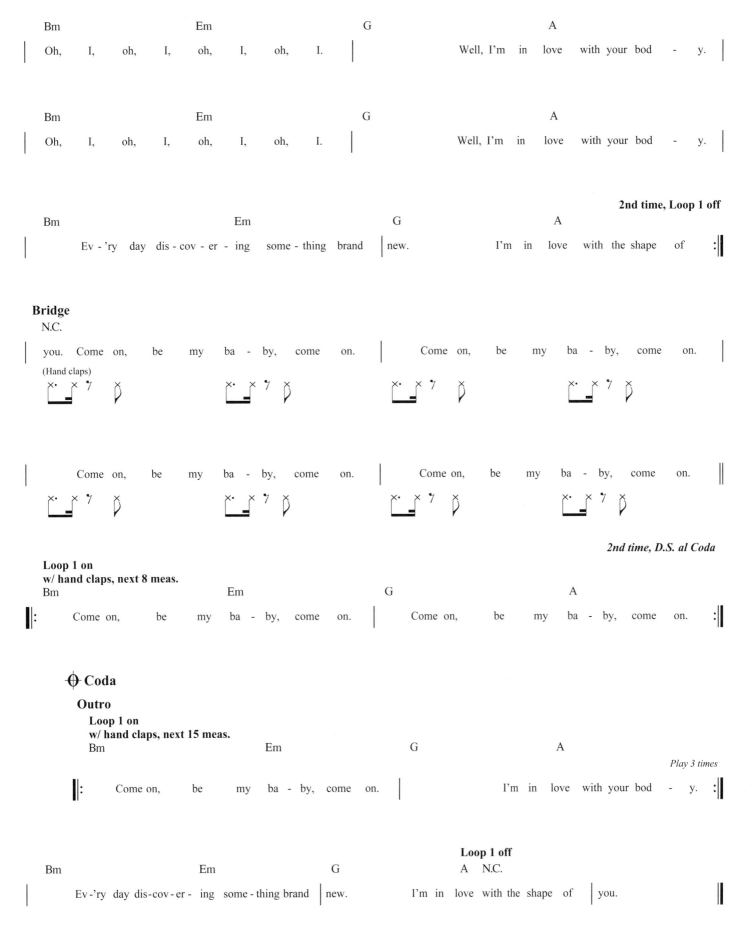

Bm   **Em**   **G**   **A**

Oh, I, oh, I, oh, I, oh, I.   Well, I'm in love with your bod - y.

Bm   **Em**   **G**   **A**

Oh, I, oh, I, oh, I, oh, I.   Well, I'm in love with your bod - y.

2nd time, Loop 1 off

Bm   **Em**   **G**   **A**

Ev - 'ry day dis - cov - er - ing some - thing brand new.   I'm in love with the shape of

Bridge

N.C.

you. Come on, be my ba - by, come on.   Come on, be my ba - by, come on.

(Hand claps)

Come on, be my ba - by, come on.   Come on, be my ba - by, come on.

2nd time, D.S. al Coda

Loop 1 on
w/ hand claps, next 8 meas.
Bm   **Em**   **G**   **A**

Come on, be my ba - by, come on.   Come on, be my ba - by, come on.

⊕ Coda

Outro
Loop 1 on
w/ hand claps, next 15 meas.
Bm   **Em**   **G**   **A**

Play 3 times

Come on, be my ba - by, come on.   I'm in love with your bod - y.

Loop 1 off

Bm   **Em**   **G**   **A**   **N.C.**

Ev - 'ry day dis - cov - er - ing some - thing brand new.   I'm in love with the shape of you.

Additional Lyrics

2. One week in, we let the story begin, we're going out on our first date.
You and me are thrifty, so go "all you can eat," fill up your bag and I fill up a plate.
We talk for hours and hours about sweet and the sour, and how your family's doing okay.
And leave and get in a taxi, then kiss in the back seat till the driver make the radio play.
And I'm singin' like...

Save Tonight

Words and Music by Eagle Eye Cherry

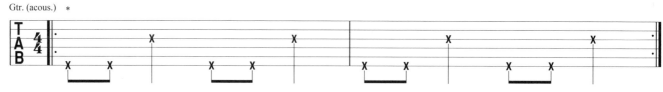

Key of Am
Intro
    Moderately fast

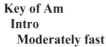

N.C.
Start Loop 1   **End Loop 1**

Gtr. (acous.) *

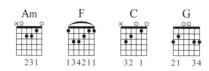

*Slap body of gtr. w/ right hand to produce kick & snare percussion effect.

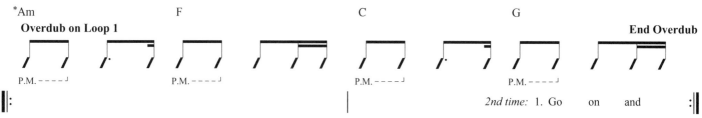

Overdub on Loop 1   **End Overdub**

P.M. - - - -   P.M. - - - -   P.M. - - - -   P.M. - - - -

2nd time: 1. Go   on   and

*See top of page for chord diagrams pertaining to rhythm slashes.

Verse
  w/ Loop 1

Am	F	C	G	Am	F	C	G
close	the	cur - tains,	'cause all we	need	is	can - dle - light.	You and
log	on	the fire,	and it	burns	like me	for you.	To - mor -

Am	F	C	G	Am	F	C	G
me,	and a	bot - tle of wine,	gon - na hold	you to-night,	ah, yeah.		Well, we
row comes	with	one de - si - re,	to take	me a - way,	it's true.		It ain't

Am	F	C	G	Am	F	C	G
know	I'm	go - ing a - way,	and how I	wish,	I wish it weren't	so.	So take this
eas - y	to	say good-bye.	Dar - lin',	please	don't start to	cry.	'Cause

Am	F	C	G	Am	F	C	G
wine,		and	drink with me.	Let's de - lay our mis - er - y.			Save to -
girl, you know I've got to go.				Lord, I wish it was - n't so.			

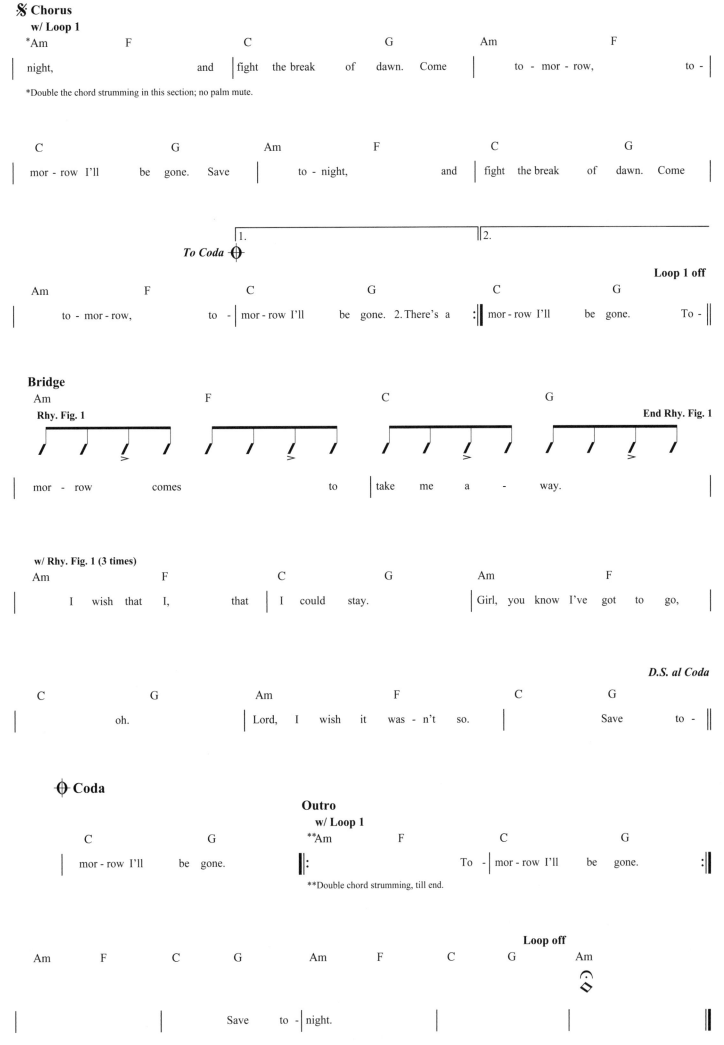

Seven Nation Army

Words and Music by Jack White

Open A tuning:
(low to high) E-A-E-A-C#-E

Key of Em
Intro
Moderately

4th time: 1. I'm gon - na

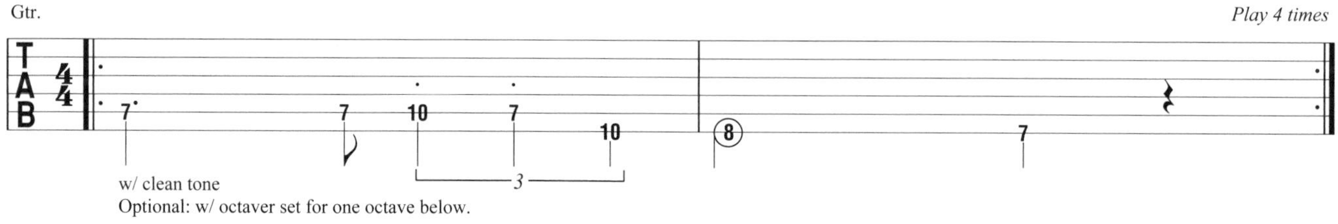

Verse
w/ Loop 1

N.C. (Em)   (C)   (B)   (Em)   (C)   (B)

fight 'em off.   A sev - en na - tion   ar - my could-n't hold me   back.   They're gon - na

2., 3. *See additional lyrics*

(Em)   (C)   (B)   (Em)   (C)   (B)

rip it off,   tak - ing their   time right be - hind my   back.   And I'm

(Em)   (C)   (B)   (Em)   (C)   (B)

talk - ing to my - self at night   be - cause I can't for - get.

Loop 1 off

(Em)   (C)   (B)   (Em)   (C)   (B)

Back and forth through my   mind   be - hind a cig - a - rette.   And the

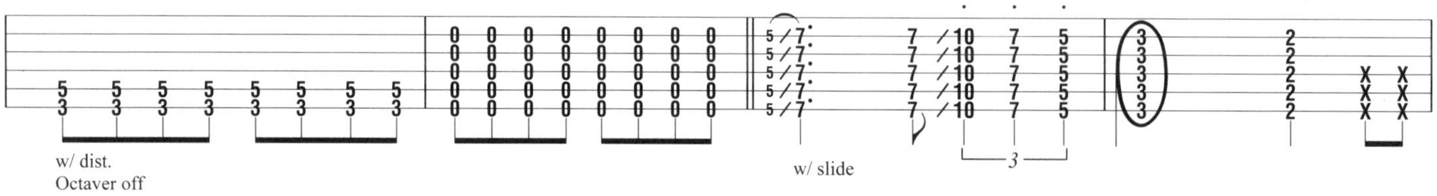

Interlude
Loop 1 on

mes - sage com - ing from my   eyes   says   leave it a - lone.

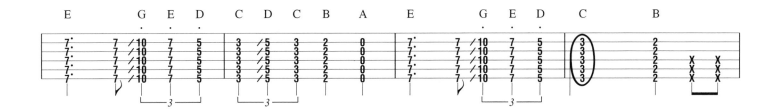

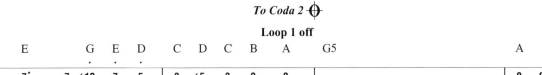

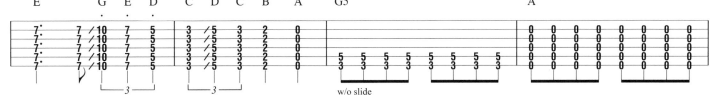

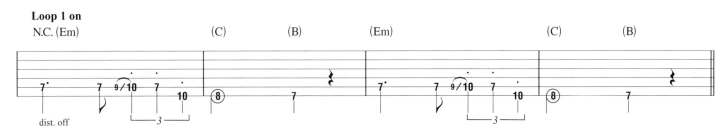

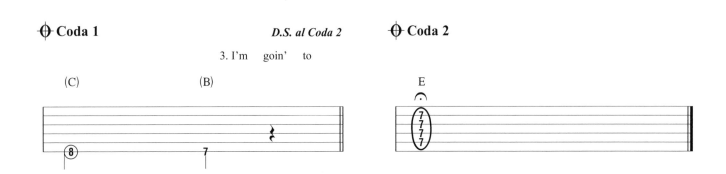

Additional Lyrics

2. Don't wanna hear about it, ev'ry single one's got a story to tell.
   Ev'ryone knows about it, from the Queen of England to the hounds of hell.
   And if I catch it coming back my way, I'm gonna serve it to you.
   And that ain't what you want to hear, but that's what I'll do.
   And the feeling coming from my bones says find a home.

3. I'm goin' to Wichita, far from this opera forevermore.
   I'm gonna work the straw, make the sweat drip out of every pore.
   And I'm bleeding, and I'm bleeding, and I'm bleeding right before the Lord.
   All the words are gonna bleed from me and I will think no more.
   And the stains coming from my blood tell me go back home.

Simple Man

Words and Music by Ronnie Van Zant and Gary Rossington

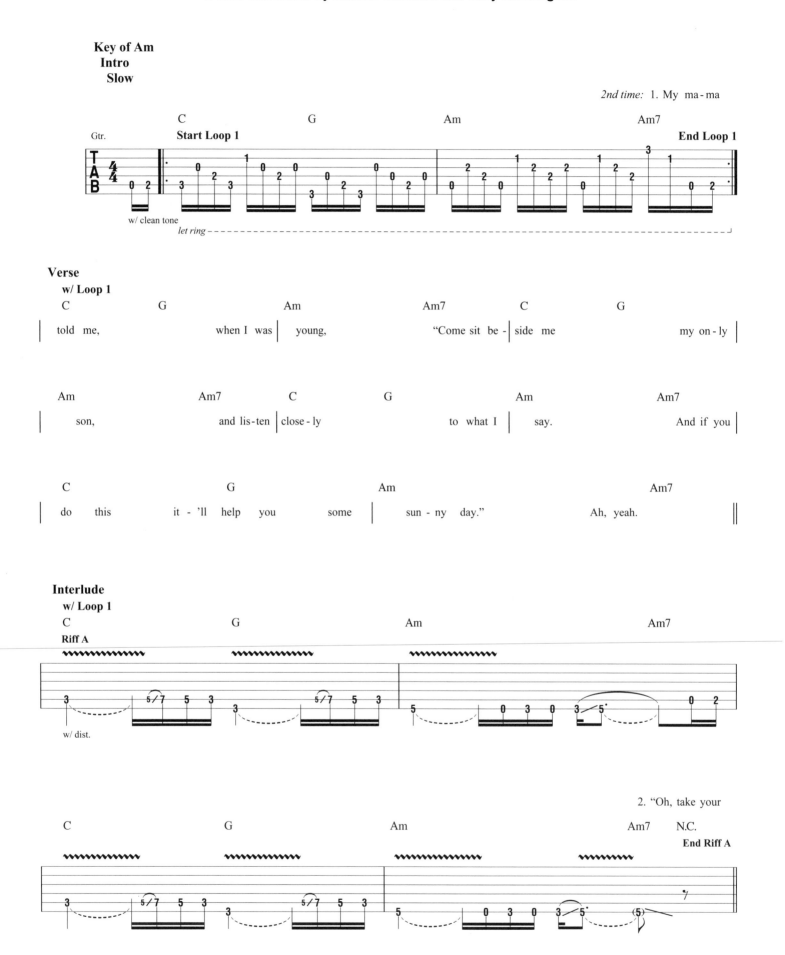

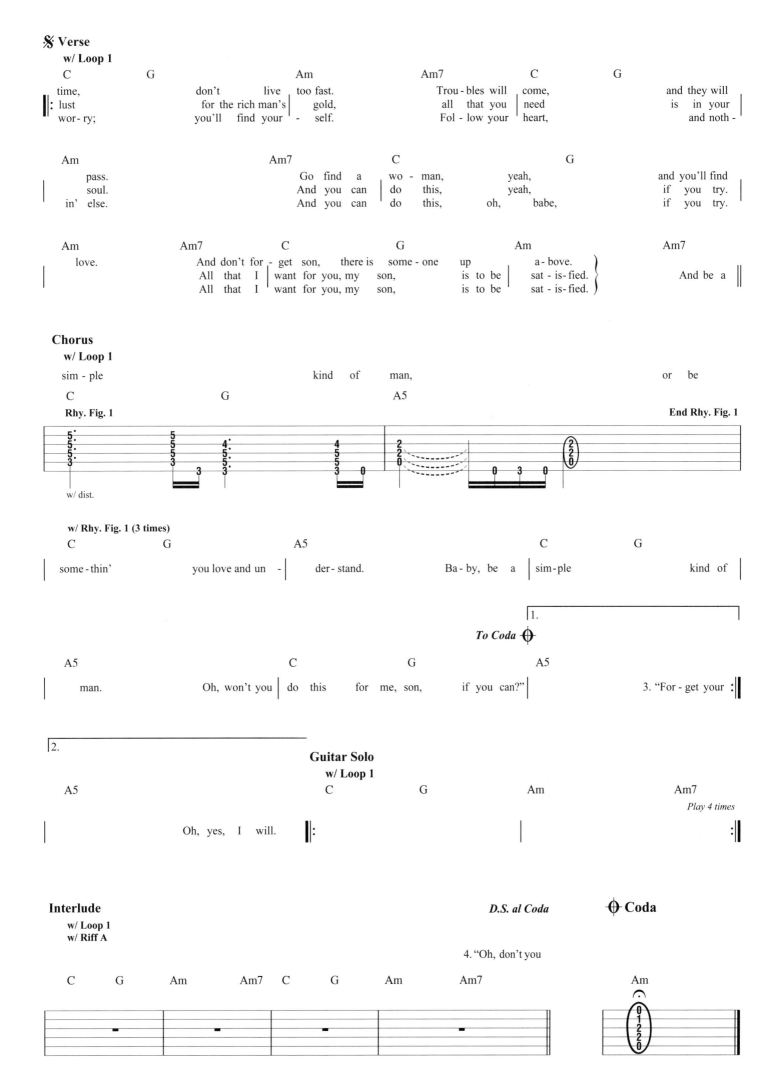

Slow Dancing in a Burning Room

Words and Music by John Mayer

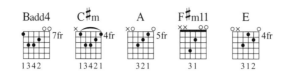

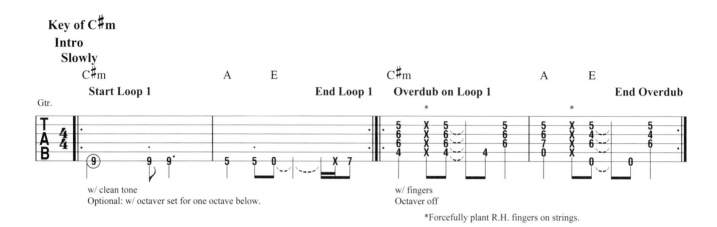

Key of C♯m
Intro
Slowly

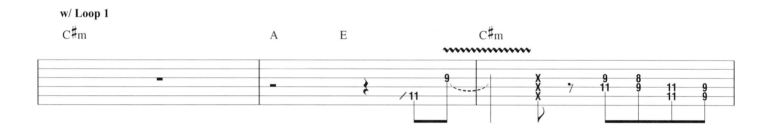

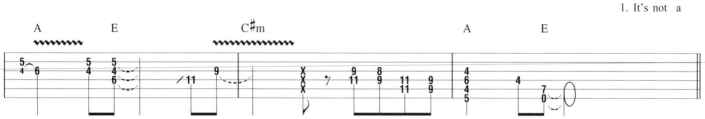

1. It's not a

% Verse
w/ Loop 1

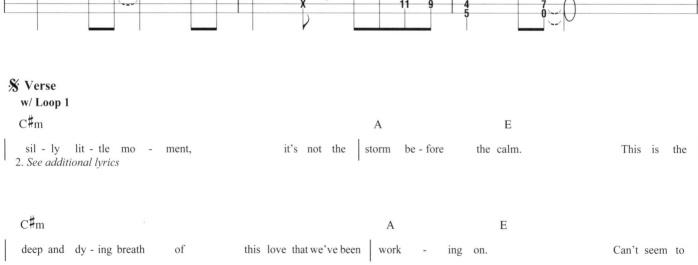

C♯m   A   E

sil - ly lit - tle mo - ment,   it's not the | storm be - fore   the calm.   This is the
2. *See additional lyrics*

C♯m   A   E

deep and dy - ing breath   of   this love that we've been | work - ing on.   Can't seem to

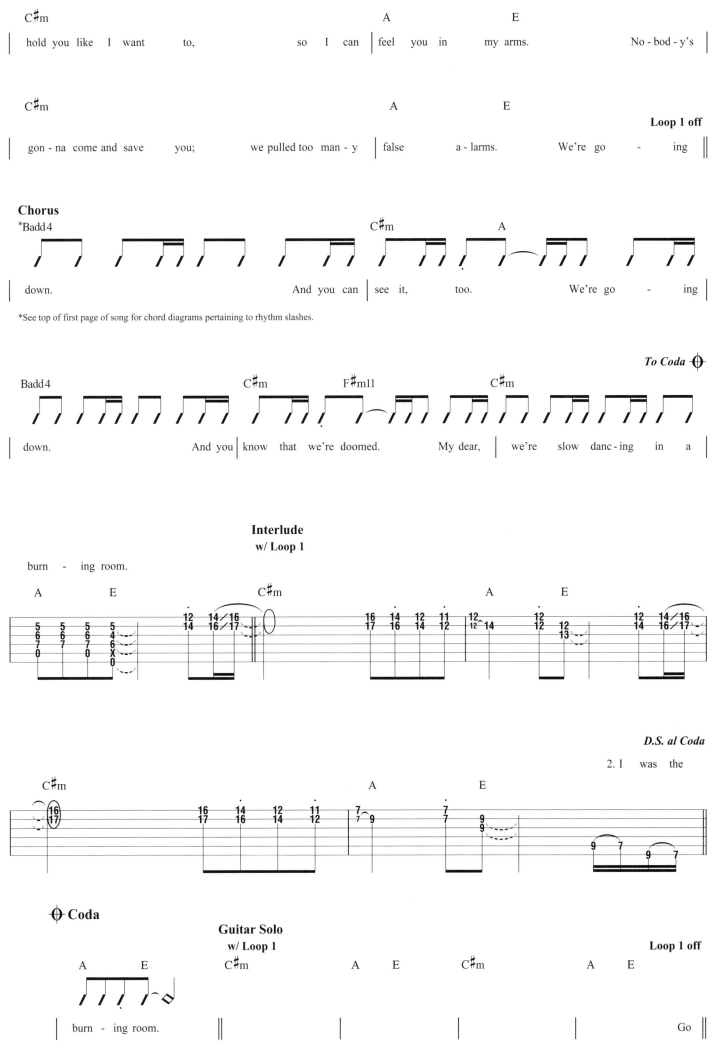

Bridge

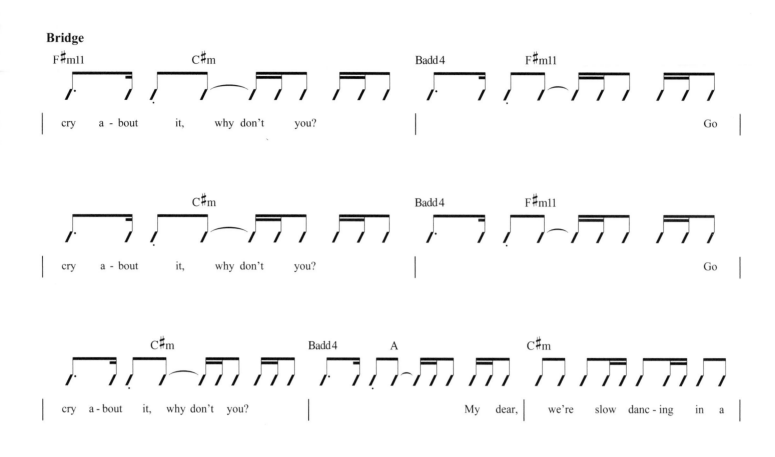

cry a - bout it, why don't you?   Go

cry a - bout it, why don't you?   Go

cry a - bout it, why don't you?   My dear,   we're   slow danc - ing   in a

Outro
Loop 1 on

burn - ing room.

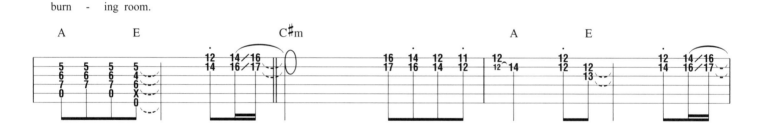

Loop 1 off

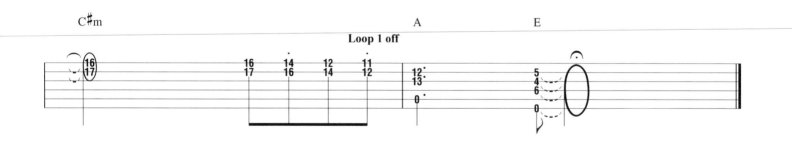

Additional Lyrics

2. I was the one you always dreamed of,
   You were the one I tried to draw.
   How dare you say it's nothing to me?
   Baby, you're the only light I ever saw.
   I'll make the most of all the sadness,
   You'll be a bitch because you can.
   You try to hit me just to hurt me so you
   Leave me feeling dirty 'cause you can't understand.

Smells Like Teen Spirit

Words and Music by Kurt Cobain, Krist Novoselic and Dave Grohl

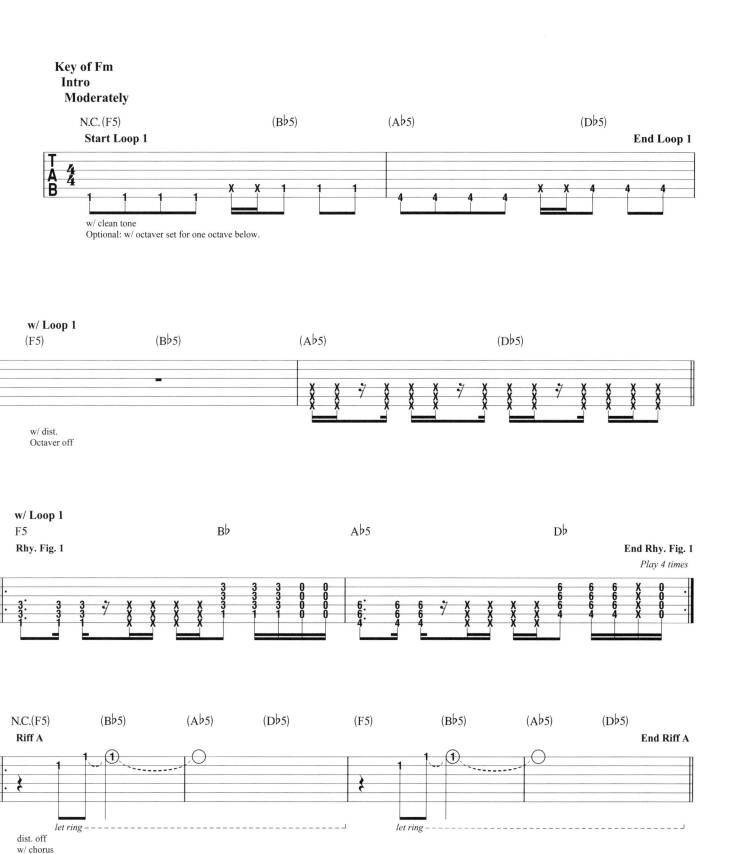

Verse

w/ Loop 1

w/ Riff A

N.C.(F5)   (Bb5)   (Ab5)   (Db5)   (F5)   (Bb5)   (Ab5)   (Db5)

1. Load up on guns and bring your friends. It's fun to lose and to pre-tend.
2. I'm worse at what I do best, and for this gift I feel blessed.

(F5)   (Bb5)   (Ab5)   (Db5)   (F5)   (Bb5)   (Ab5)   (Db5)

She's o-ver-bored and self-as-sured. Oh no, I know a dirt-y word.
Our lit-tle group has al-ways been, and al-ways will un-til the end.

𝄋 Pre-Chorus

w/ Loop 1

Hel-lo, hel-lo, hel-lo, how low? Hel-lo, hel-lo, hel-lo, how low?

(F5)   (Bb5)   (Ab5)   (Db5)   (F5)   (Bb5)   (Ab5)   (Db5)

Riff B   **End Riff B**

w/ slight dist.
let ring - ⌐

w/ Riff B

(F5)   (Bb5)   (Ab5)   (Db5)   (F5)   (Bb5)   (Ab5)   (Db5)

Hel-lo, hel-lo, hel-lo, how low? Hel-lo, hel-lo, hel-lo. With the lights

Chorus

w/ Loop 1

w/ Rhy. Fig. 1 (6 times)

F5   Bb   Ab5   Db   F5   Bb   Ab5   Db

out it's less dan - g'rous. Here we are now, en-ter-tain us. I feel stu -

F5   Bb   Ab5   Db   F5   Bb   Ab5   Db

- pid and con-ta - gious. Here we are now, en-ter-tain us. A mul-la -

To Coda ⊕

F5   Bb   Ab5   Db   F5   Bb   Ab5   Db

- to, an al-bi - no, a mos-qui - to, my li-bi - do. Yeah,

Bridge

Loop 1 off

yay,   yay.

F5   E5 F5 Gb5   N.C.   F5   E5 F5 Bb5   Ab5   F5   E5 F5 Gb5   N.C.

w/ dist.

88

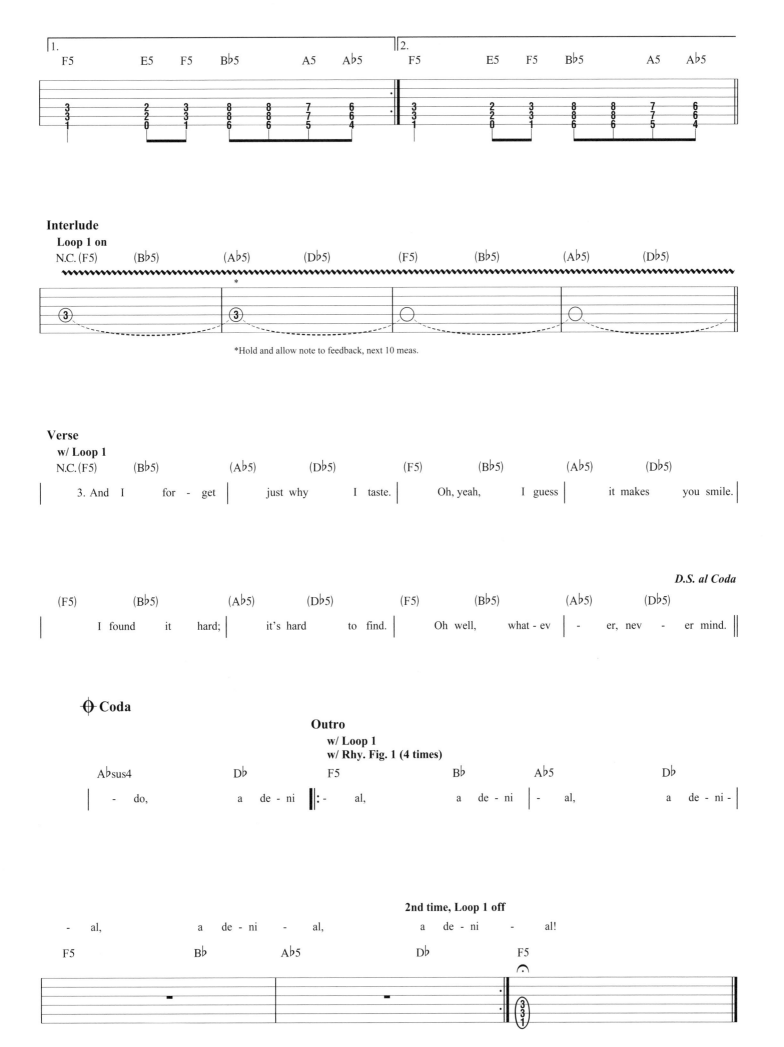

Stand by Me

Words and Music by Jerry Leiber, Mike Stoller and Ben E. King

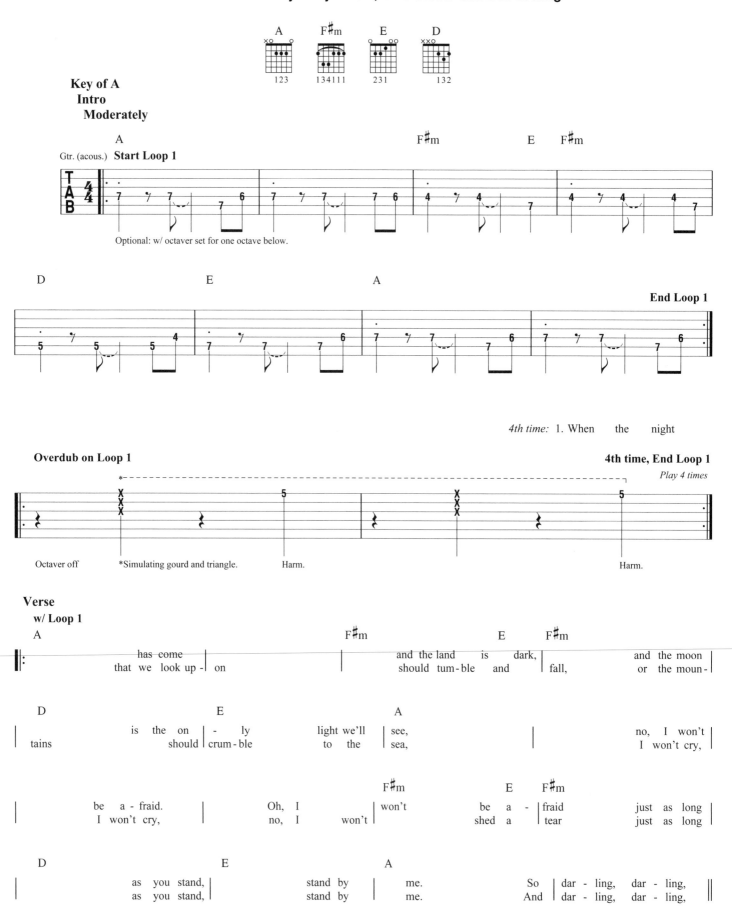

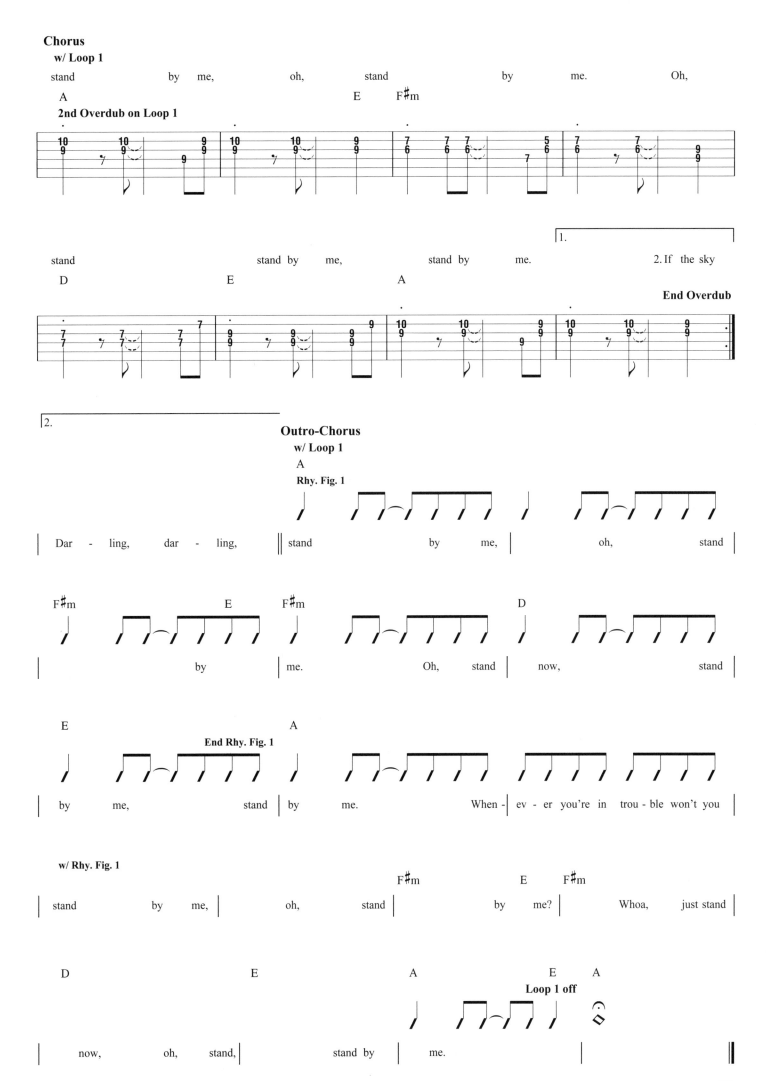

Stay with Me

Words and Music by Sam Smith, James Napier, William Edward Phillips, Tom Petty and Jeff Lynne

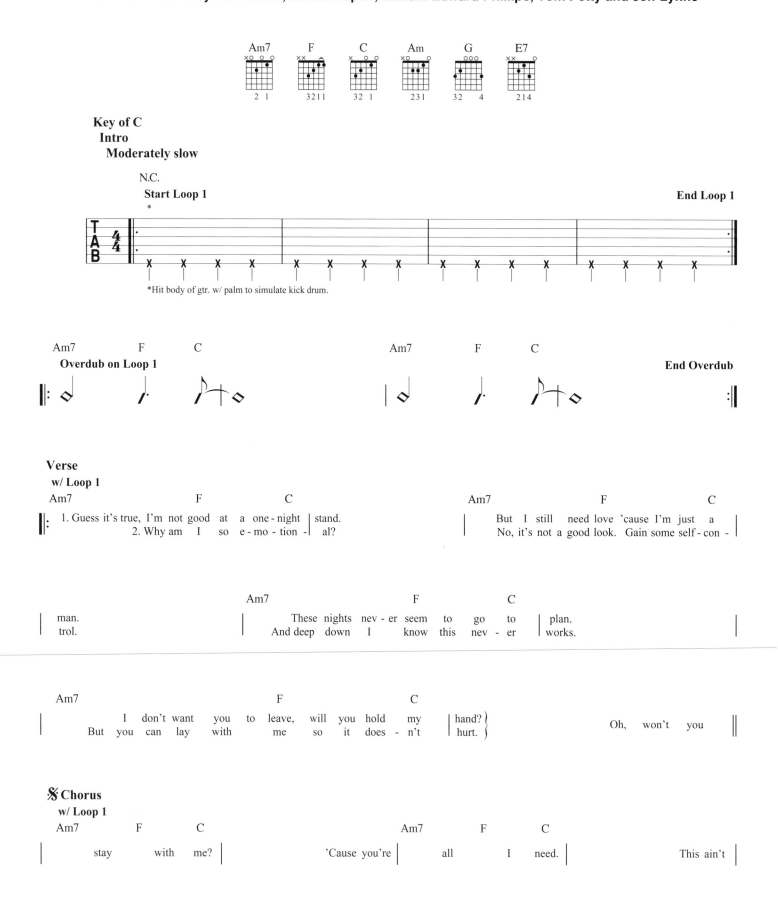

Key of C
Intro
Moderately slow

*Hit body of gtr. w/ palm to simulate kick drum.

Verse

Am7   F   C
1. Guess it's true, I'm not good at a one-night stand.
2. Why am I so e-mo-tion-al?

But I still need love 'cause I'm just a
No, it's not a good look. Gain some self-con-

man.
trol.

Am7   F   C
These nights nev-er seem to go to plan.
And deep down I know this nev-er works.

Am7   F   C
I don't want you to leave, will you hold my hand?
But you can lay with me so it does-n't hurt.

Oh, won't you

Chorus
w/ Loop 1

Am7   F   C
stay with me?

Am7   F   C
'Cause you're all I need.

This ain't

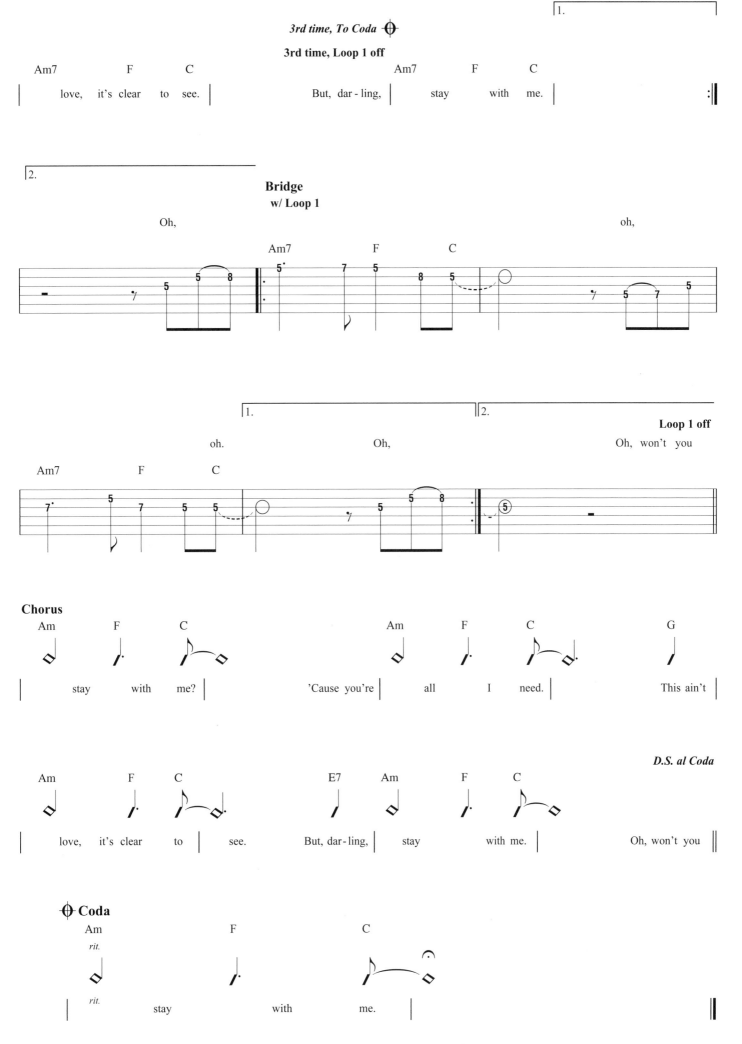

Stir It Up

Words and Music by Bob Marley

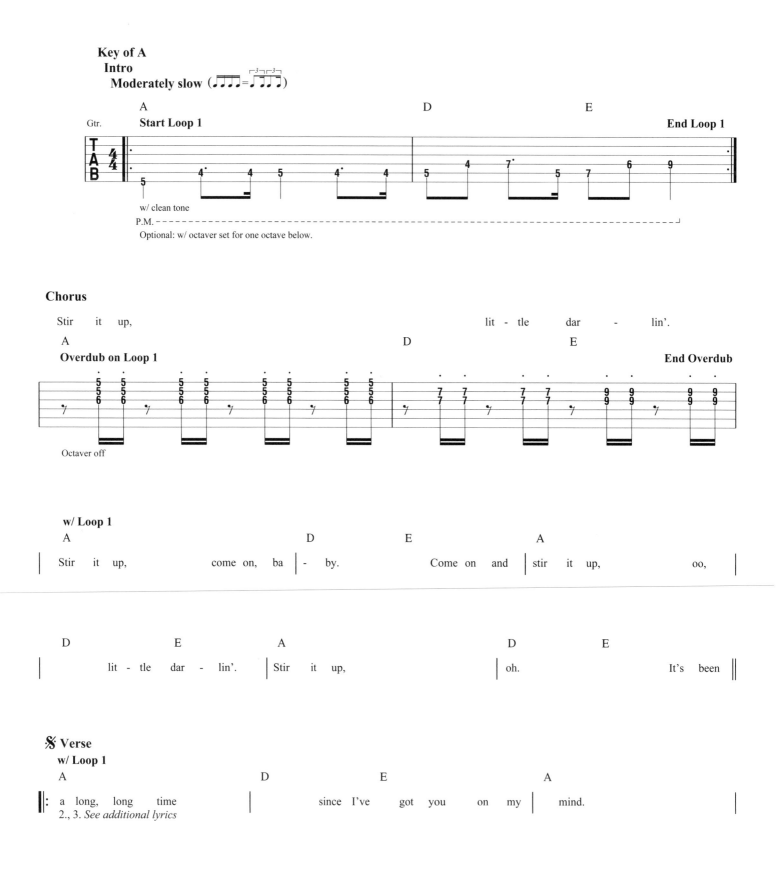

D	E	A		D	E

And | now you are here.   I say | it's o - kay to |

A		D	E

see what - a we will do, ba - by, | just me and you. Come on and ‖

Chorus
w/ Loop 1

A		D	E	A

stir it up,   I wan-na say, | lit - tle dar - lin', yeah. | Stir it up,   come on, ba-

D	E	A		D	E

- by.   Come on and | stir it up,   yeah, | lit - tle dar - lin'. |

| 1. | | 2. |

To Coda ⊕   *D.S. al Coda*

A		D	E	D	E

Stir it up,   oh. | :‖ Whoa,   mm. 3. And then ‖

⊕ **Coda**

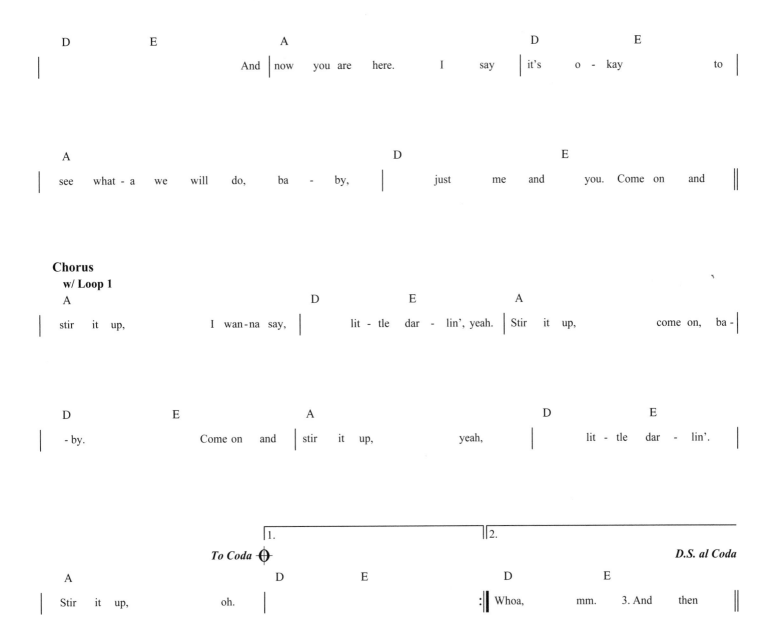

Loop 1 off

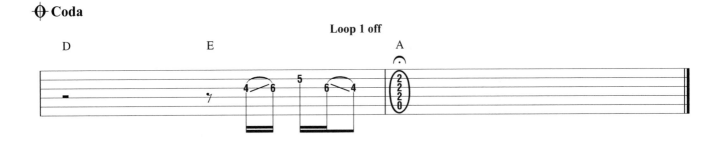

Additional Lyrics

2. I'll push the wood, and I'll blaze your fire.
   Then I satisfy your all desire.
   Said I stir it, yeah, every minute.
   All you've got to do, baby, is keep it in it, and...

3. And then quench me when I'm thirsty.
   Come on, cool me down, baby, when I'm hot.
   Your recipe, darlin', is so tasty.
   And you sure can stir the pot, so...

Sunday Morning

Words and Music by Adam Levine and Jesse Carmichael

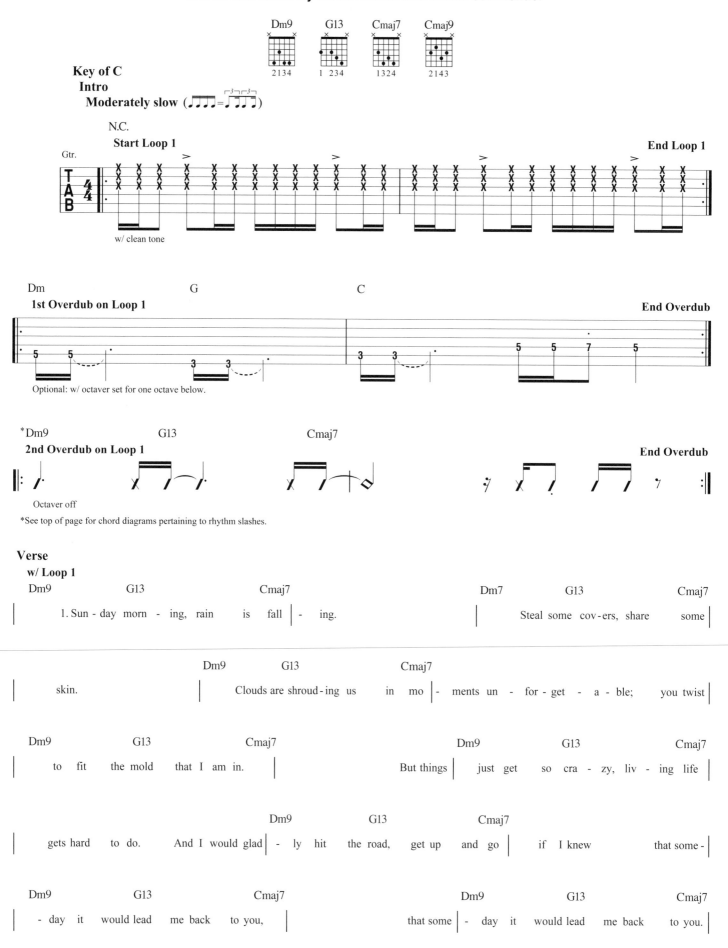

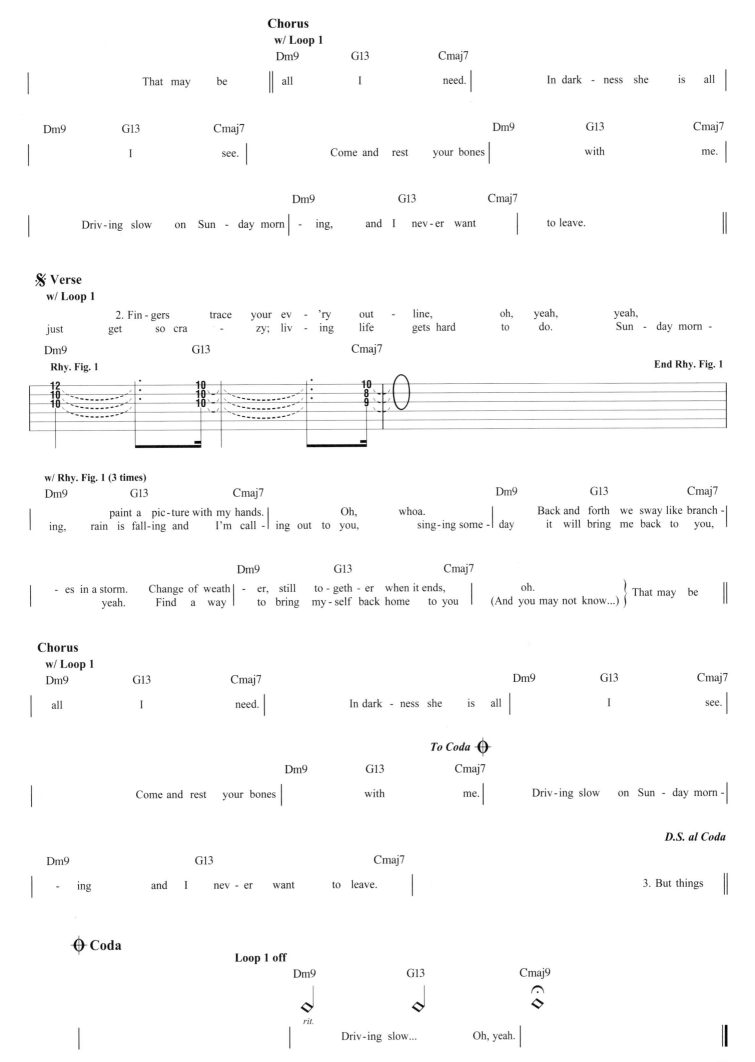

Sunny

Words and Music by Bobby Hebb

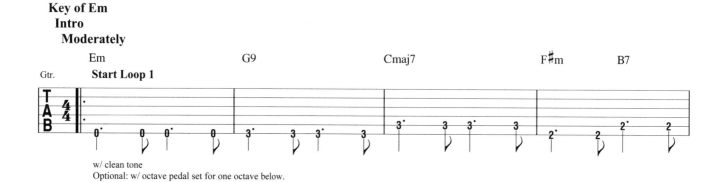

Key of Em
Intro
Moderately

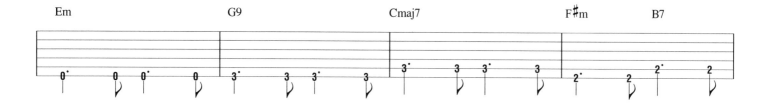

w/ clean tone
Optional: w/ octave pedal set for one octave below.

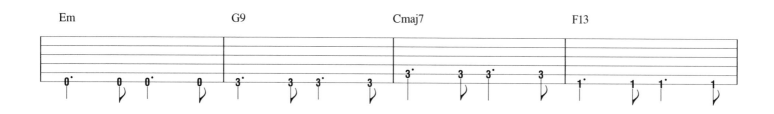

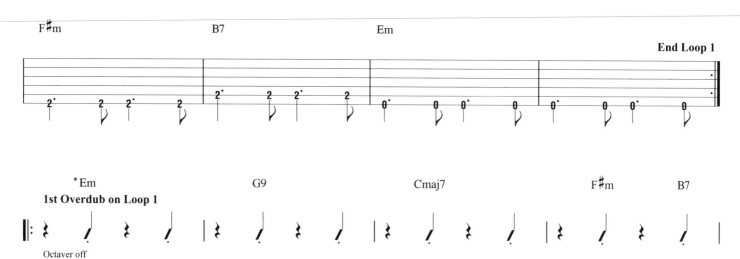

Octaver off

*See top of page for chord diagrams pertaining to rhythm slashes.

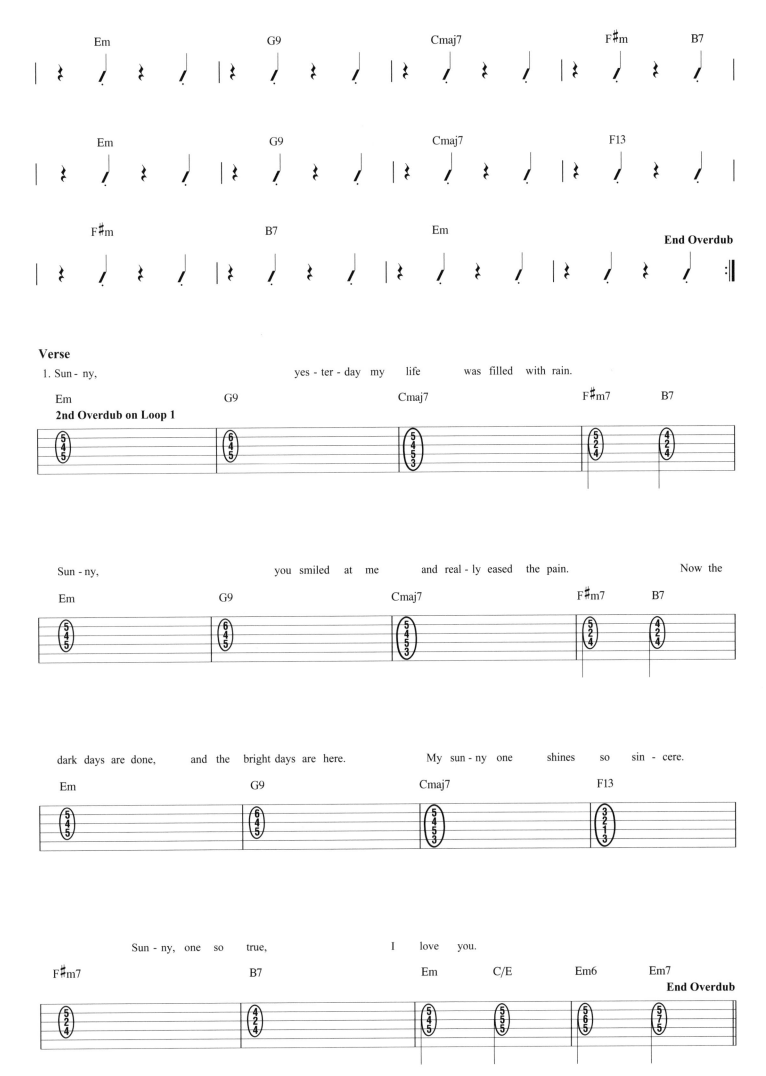

Verse
w/ Loop 1

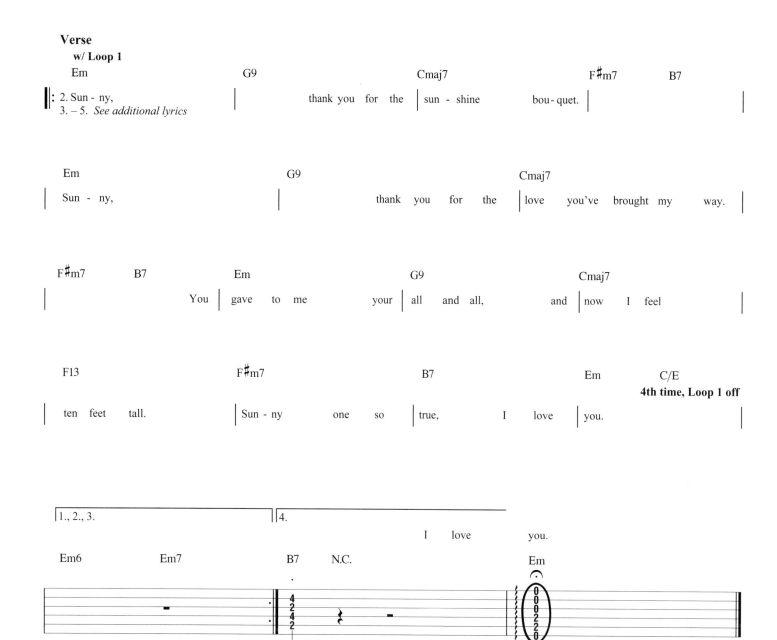

Em   **G9**   **Cmaj7**   **F#m7**   **B7**

2. Sun - ny,
3. – 5. *See additional lyrics*

thank you for the | sun - shine bou-quet. |

Em   **G9**   **Cmaj7**

Sun - ny,   thank you for the | love you've brought my way. |

F#m7   **B7**   **Em**   **G9**   **Cmaj7**

You | gave to me your | all and all, and | now I feel

F13   **F#m7**   **B7**   **Em**   **C/E**

4th time, Loop 1 off

ten feet tall. | Sun - ny one so | true, I love | you. |

1., 2., 3. | 4.

I love you.

Em6   **Em7**   **B7**   **N.C.**   **Em**

Additional Lyrics

3. Sunny, thank you for the truth you've let me see.
Sunny, thank you for the facts from A to Z.
My life was torn like wind-blown sand,
Then a rock was formed when we held hands.
Sunny, one so true, I love you.

4. Sunny, thank you for that smile upon your face.
Sunny, thank you, thank you for that gleam that flows with grace.
You're my spark of nature's fire;
You're my sweet complete desire.
Sunny, one so true, yes, I love you.

5. Sunny, yesterday all my life was filled with rain.
And Sunny, you smiled at me and really, really eased the pain.
Now the dark days are done and the bright days are here.
My sunny one shines so sincere.
Sunny, one so true, I love you.

100

Undone - The Sweater Song

Words and Music by Rivers Cuomo

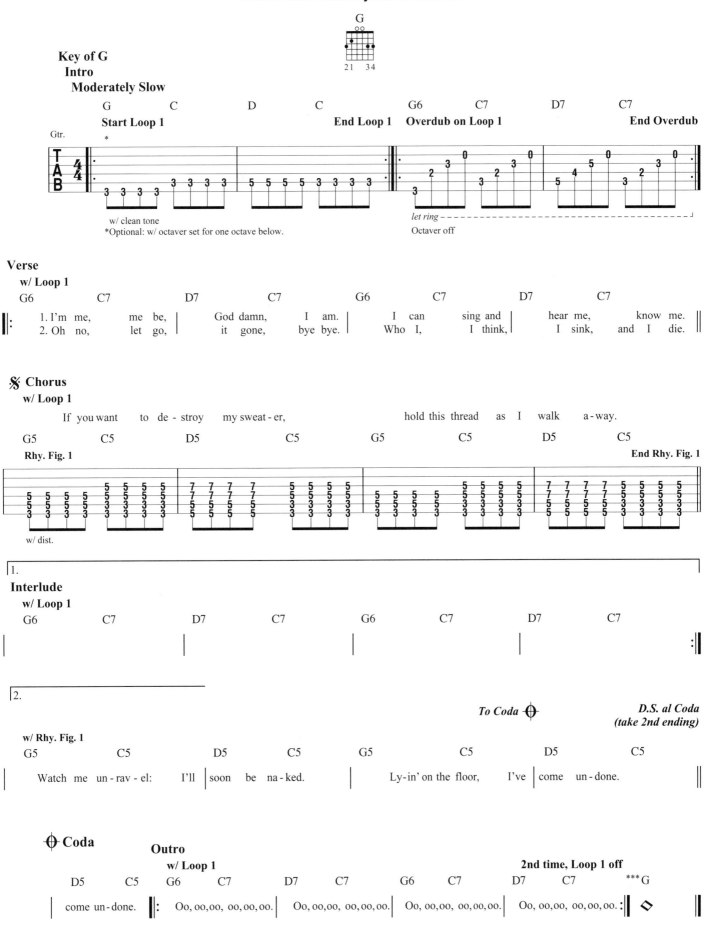

Key of G
Intro
Moderately Slow

Verse

1. I'm me, me be, God damn, I am. I can sing and hear me, know me.
2. Oh no, let go, it gone, bye bye. Who I, I think, I sink, and I die.

Chorus

If you want to de-stroy my sweat-er, hold this thread as I walk a-way.

Interlude

1.

2.

To Coda / *D.S. al Coda (take 2nd ending)*

Watch me un-rav-el: I'll soon be na-ked. Ly-in' on the floor, I've come un-done.

Coda

Outro

come un-done. Oo, oo,oo, oo,oo,oo. Oo, oo,oo, oo,oo,oo. Oo, oo,oo, oo,oo,oo. Oo, oo,oo, oo,oo,oo.

***See top of page for chord diagram pertaining to rhythm slash.

Takin' Care of Business

Words and Music by Randy Bachman

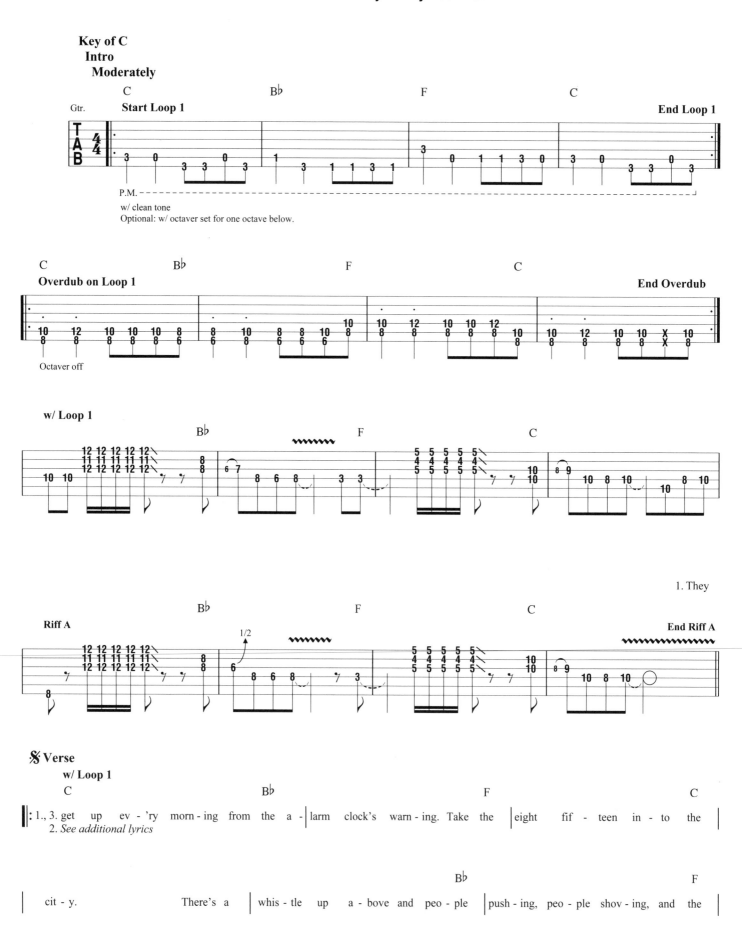

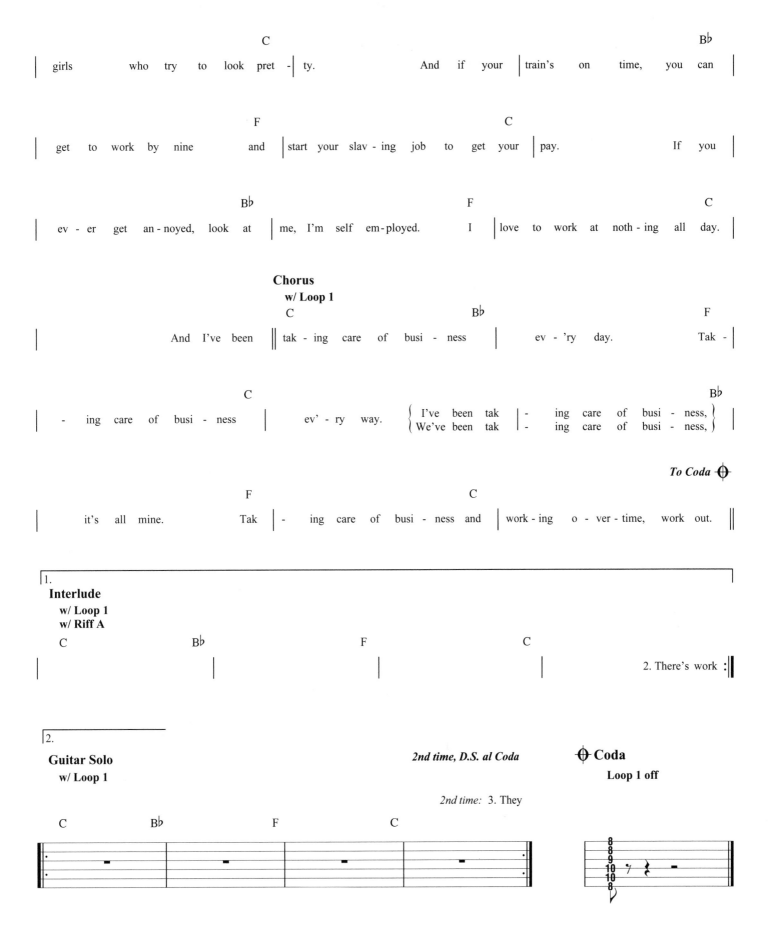

		C											Bb

girls   who   try   to   look   pret - | ty.   And   if   your | train's   on   time,   you   can |

F   C

get   to   work   by   nine   and | start   your   slav - ing   job   to   get   your | pay.   If   you |

Bb   F   C

ev - er   get   an - noyed,   look   at | me,   I'm   self   em - ployed.   I | love   to   work   at   noth - ing   all   day. |

Chorus
w/ Loop 1

C   Bb   F

And   I've   been ‖ tak - ing   care   of   busi - ness | ev - 'ry   day.   Tak - |

C   Bb

- ing   care   of   busi - ness | ev' - ry   way.   { I've   been   tak | - ing   care   of   busi - ness, }   { We've   been   tak | - ing   care   of   busi - ness, }

To Coda ⊕

F   C

it's   all   mine.   Tak | - ing   care   of   busi - ness   and | work - ing   o - ver - time,   work   out. ‖

1.

Interlude
w/ Loop 1
w/ Riff A

C   Bb   F   C

2. There's work ‖

2.

Guitar Solo
w/ Loop 1

2nd time, D.S. al Coda   ⊕ **Coda**

Loop 1 off

2nd time: 3. They

C   Bb   F   C

Additional Lyrics

2. There's work easy as fishin', you could be a musician,
    If you could make sounds loud or mellow.
    Get a second-hand guitar, chances are you'll go far
    If you get in with the right group of fellows.
    People see you having fun just a lying in the sun.
    Tell them that you like it this way.
    It's the work that we avoid and we're all self-employed.
    We love to work at nothing all day.
    And we've been...

Twist and Shout

Words and Music by Bert Russell and Phil Medley

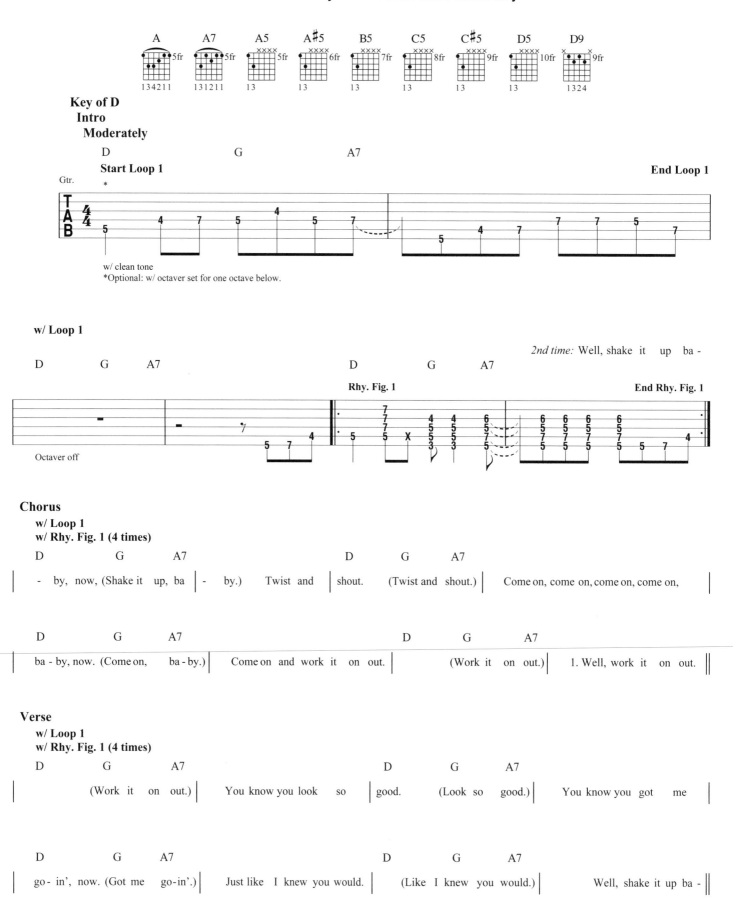

Key of D
Intro
Moderately

Chorus
w/ Loop 1
w/ Rhy. Fig. 1 (4 times)

- by, now, (Shake it up, ba - by.) Twist and shout. (Twist and shout.) Come on, come on, come on, come on,

ba - by, now. (Come on, ba - by.) Come on and work it on out. (Work it on out.) 1. Well, work it on out.

Verse
w/ Loop 1
w/ Rhy. Fig. 1 (4 times)

(Work it on out.) You know you look so good. (Look so good.) You know you got me

go- in', now. (Got me go-in'.) Just like I knew you would. (Like I knew you would.) Well, shake it up ba -

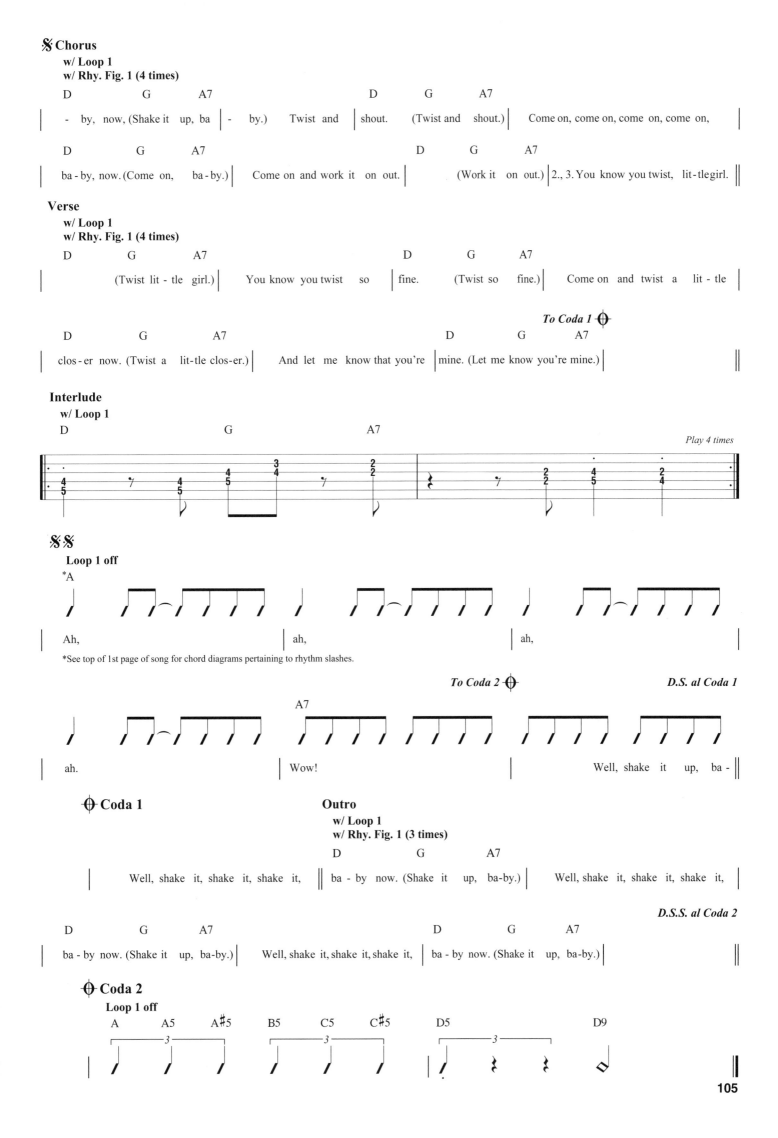

Use Somebody

Words and Music by Caleb Followill, Nathan Followill, Jared Followill and Matthew Followill

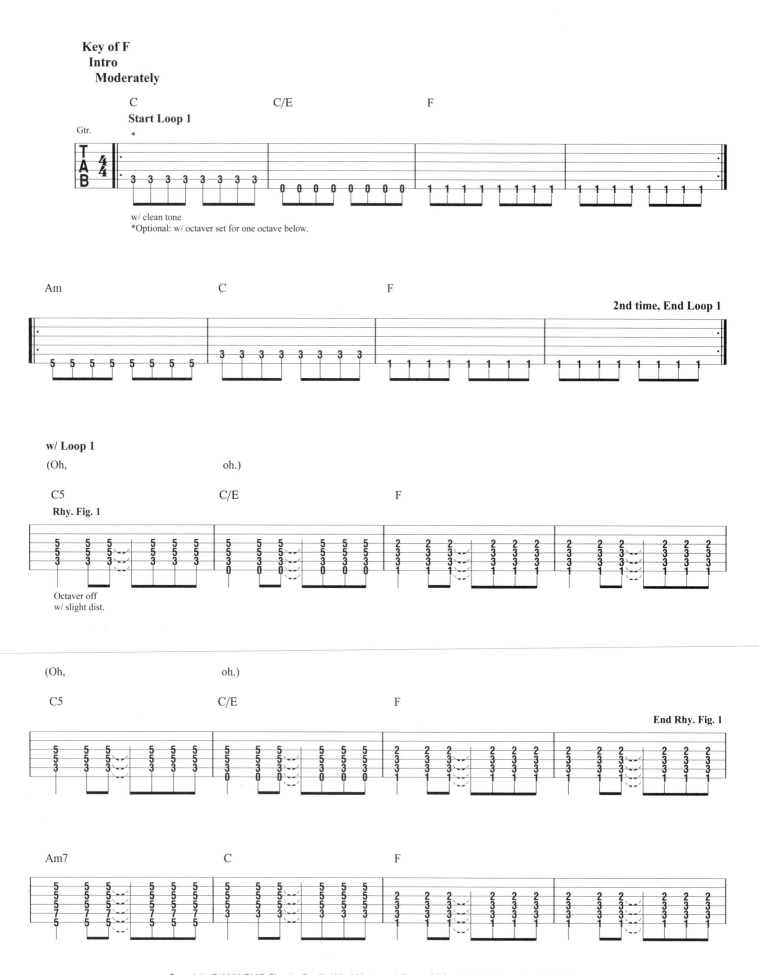

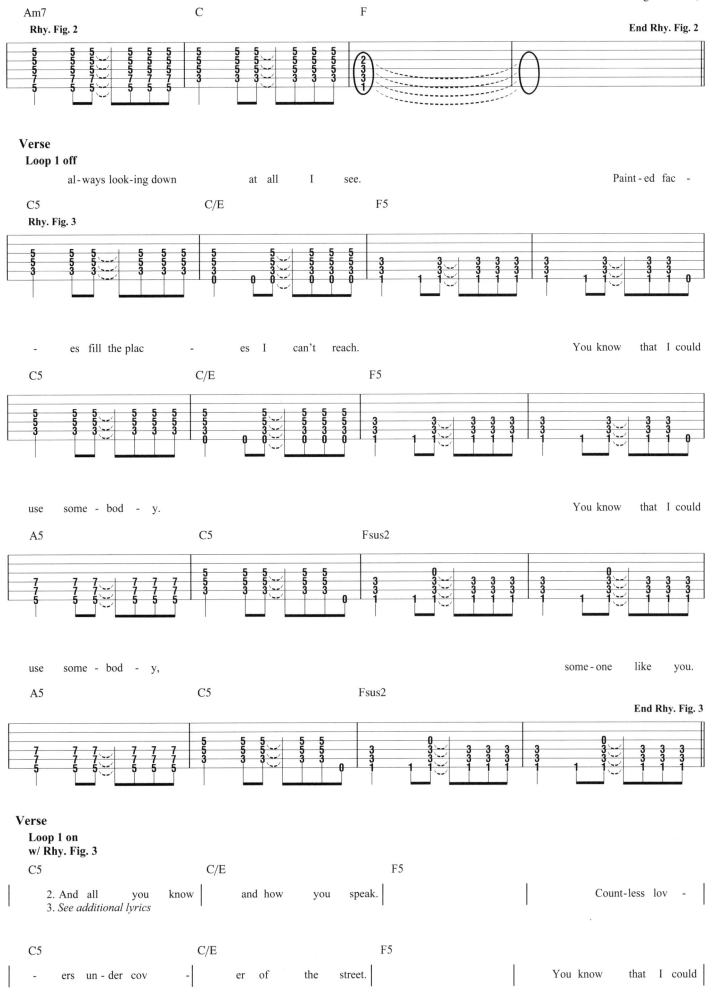

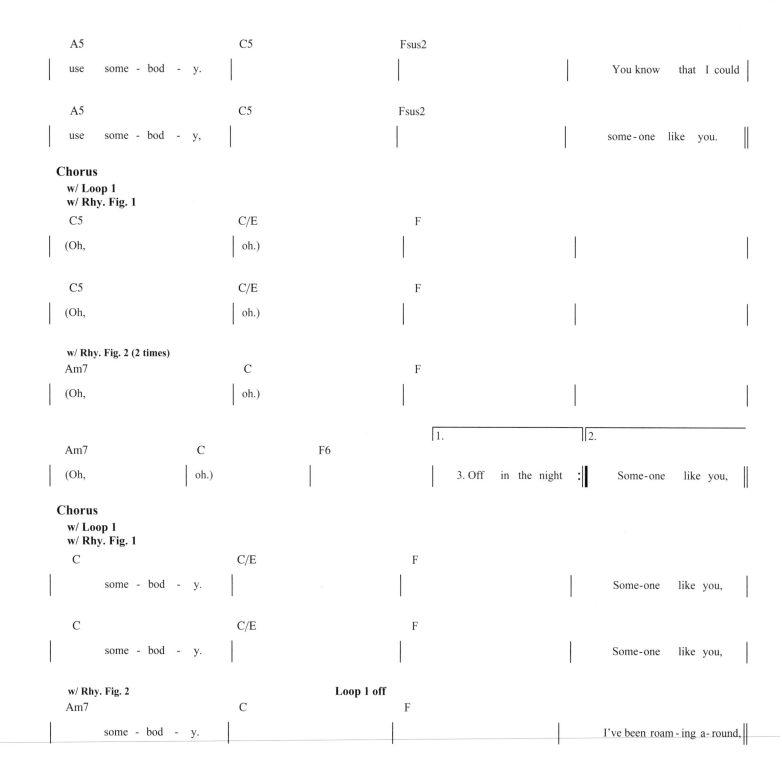

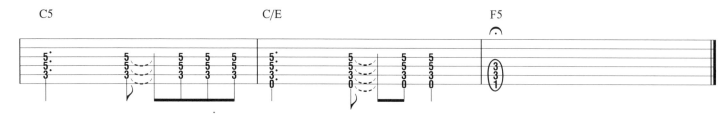

Additional Lyrics

3. Off in the night while you live it up, I'm off to sleep,
   Waging wars to shake the poet and the beat.
   I hope it's gonna make you notice.
   I hope it's gonna make you notice someone like me.

Chorus Someone like me.
   Someone like me, (somebody).

Viva La Vida

Words and Music by Guy Berryman, Jon Buckland, Will Champion and Chris Martin

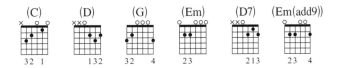

Capo I
Key of A♭ (Capoed key of G)
  Intro
    Moderately fast

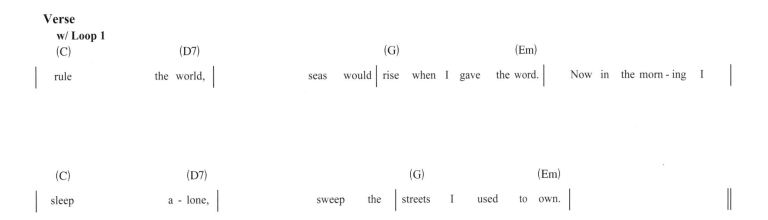

Verse
  w/ Loop 1

(C)	(D7)		(G)	(Em)	
rule	the world,	seas would	rise when I gave the word.	Now in the morn-ing I	

(C)	(D7)		(G)	(Em)	
sleep	a - lone,	sweep the	streets I used to own.		

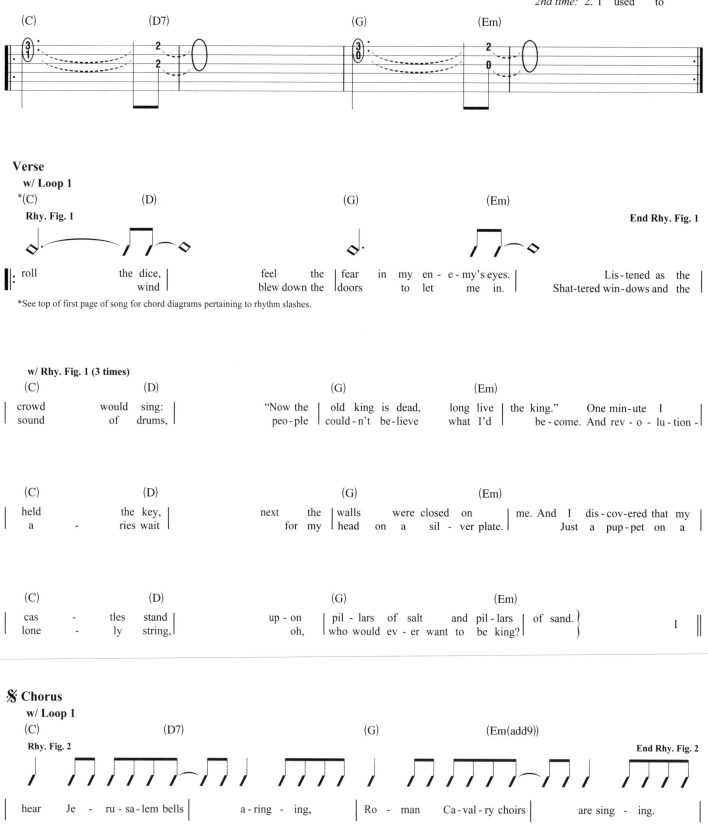
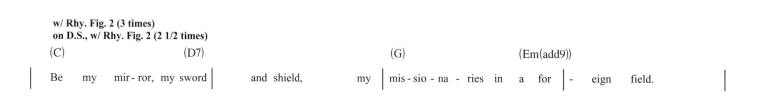

(C)   (D7)   (G)   (Em(add9))

1. For some rea-son I can't | ex - plain, | once you'd gone there was | nev - er, nev - er an hon-|
2., 3. For some rea-son I can't | ex - plain, | I | know Saint Pe - ter won't call | my name. Nev - er |

(C)   (D7) |1.   (G)   (Em(add9))

-     est word, | and that was | when I ruled the world. | |
an hon - est word, | but that was |

3. It was the wick-ed and wild

(C)   (D7)   (G)   (Em)

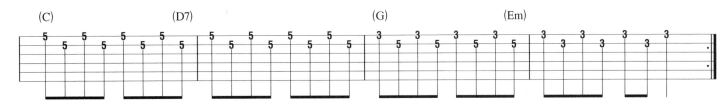

|2.

Bridge
w/ Loop 1
w/ Rhy. Fig. 1 (2 times)

(G)   (Em(add9))   (C)   (D7)   (G)   (Em)

| when I ruled the world. | Oh, oh. ‖ | | Oh, oh. | |

D.S. al Coda

(C)   (D7)   (G)   (Em)

| Oh, oh. | | Oh, oh. | | Oh, oh. ‖

⊕ **Coda**

Loop 1 off
(C)   (D7)   (G)   (Em)

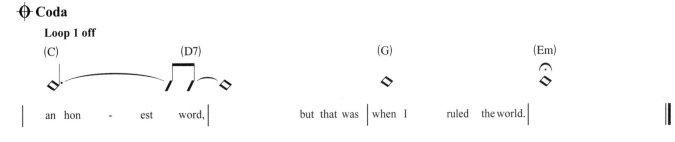

| an hon - est word, | but that was | when I ruled the world. |

Wake Me Up!

Words and Music by Aloe Blacc, Tim Bergling and Michael Einziger

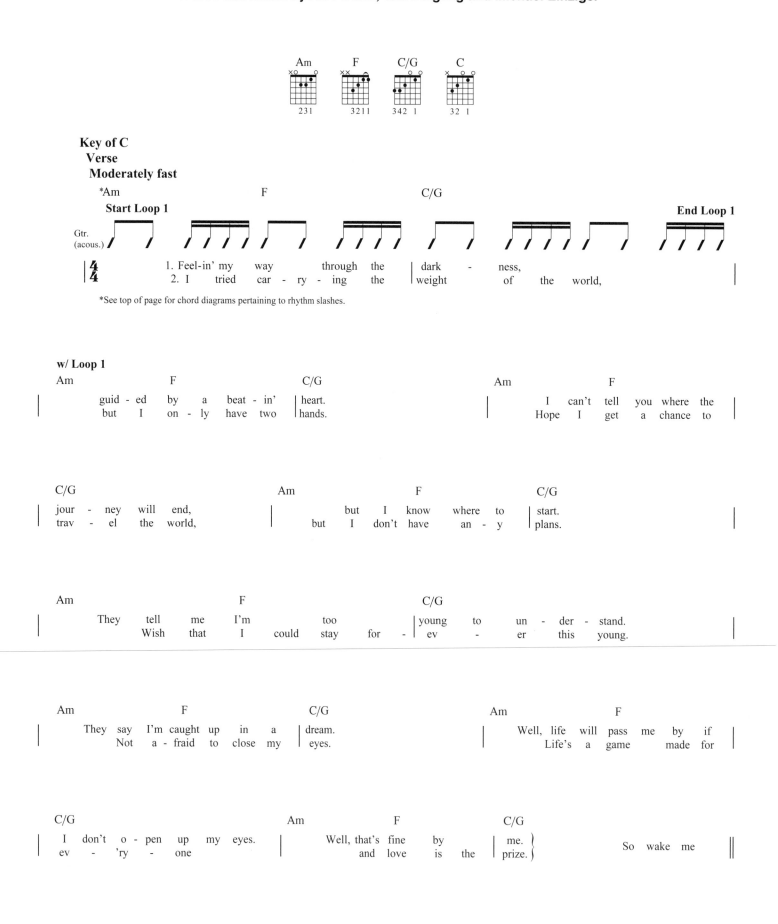

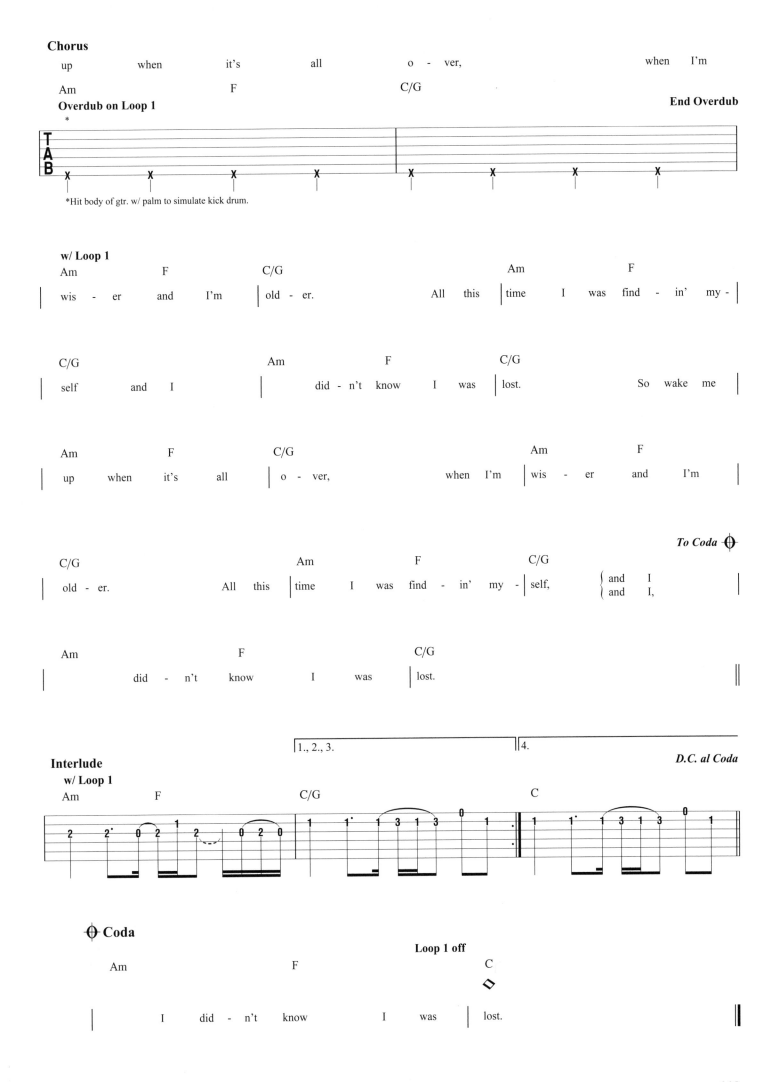

Walk on the Wild Side

Words and Music by Lou Reed

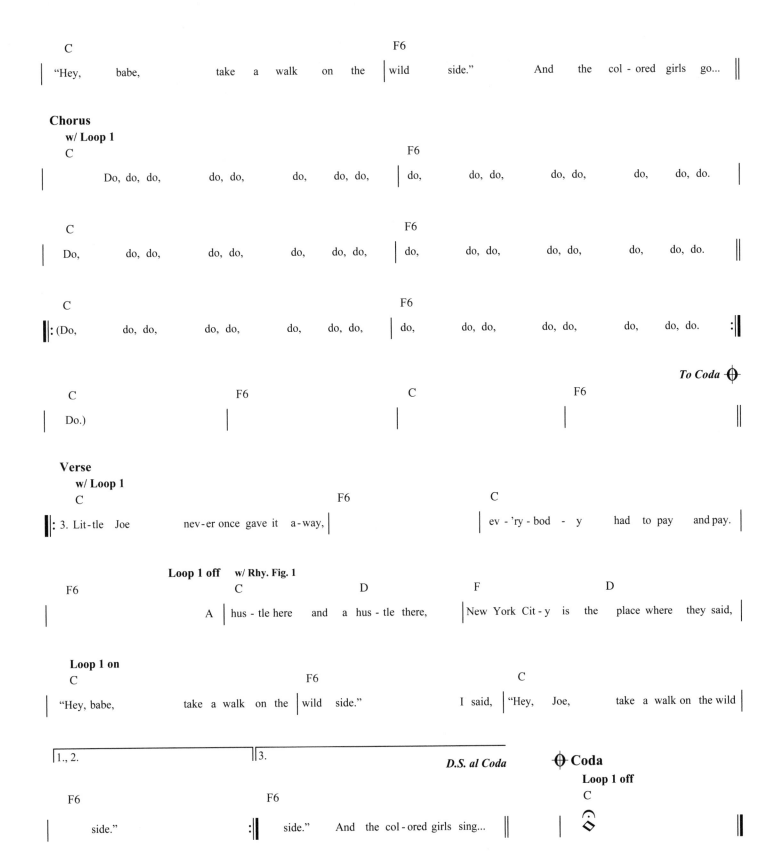

Additional Lyrics

4. Sugar plum fairies came and hit the streets
   Looking for soul food and a place to eat.
   Went to the Apollo; you should have seen them go, go, go.
   They said, "Hey, sugar, take a walk on the wild side."
   I said, "Hey babe, take a walk on the wild side."

5. Jackie is just speeding away.
   Thought she was James Dean for a day.
   Then I guess she had to crash; Valium would've helped that bash.
   She said, "Hey, babe, take a walk on the wild side."
   She said, "Hey, honey, take a walk on the wild side."

Werewolves of London

Words and Music by Warren Zevon, Waddy Wachtel and Leroy Marinell

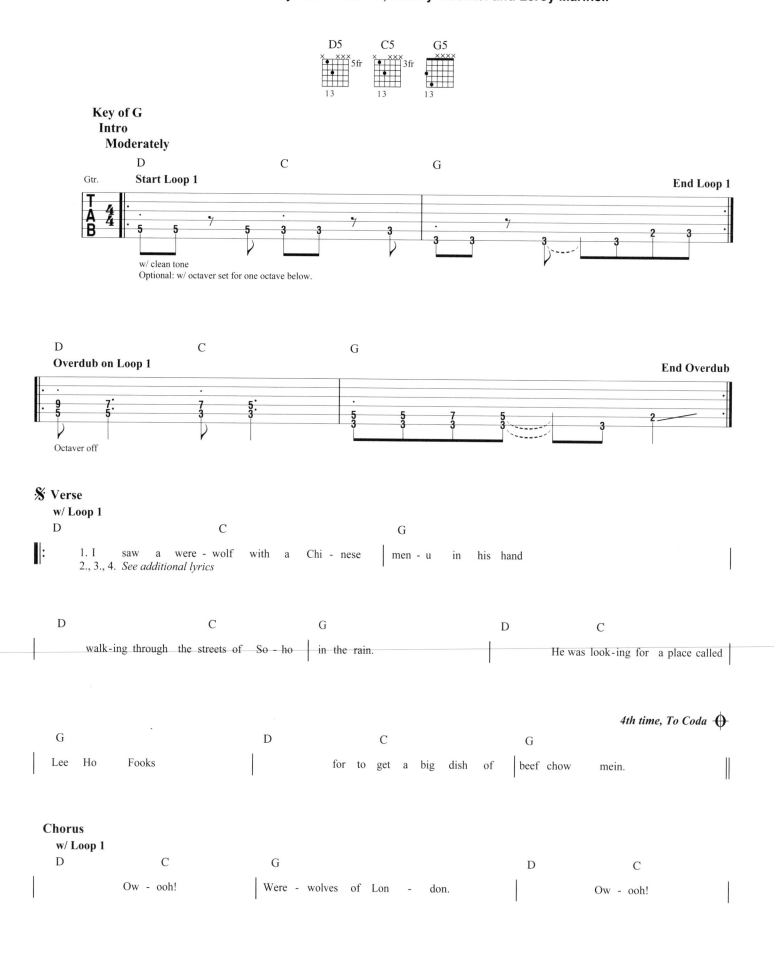

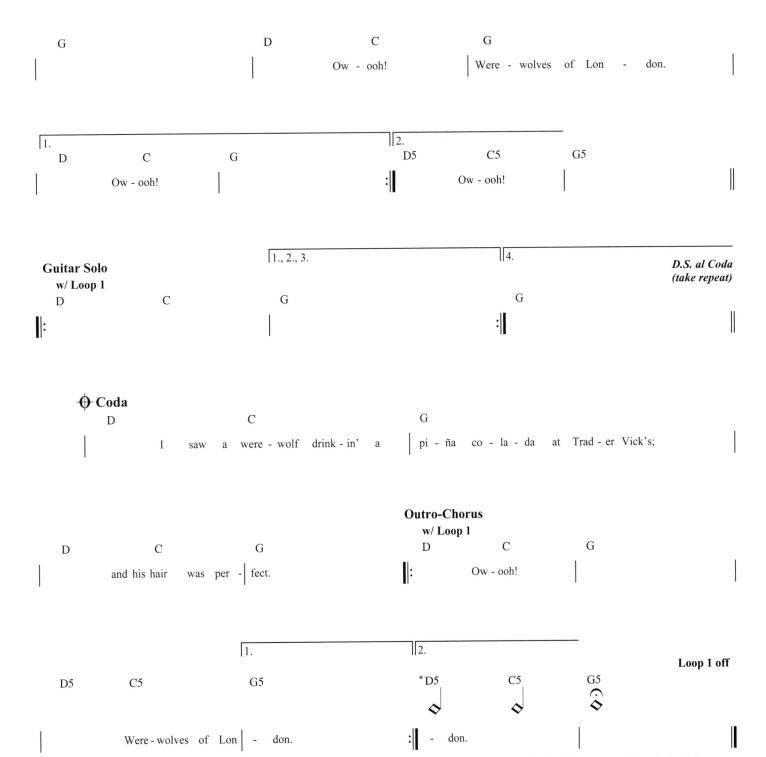

	G		D	C	G	
			Ow - ooh!		Were - wolves of Lon - don.	

1.

D	C	G	**2.** D5	C5	G5	
Ow - ooh!			Ow - ooh!			

Guitar Solo
w/ Loop 1

1., 2., 3. | **4.** | *D.S. al Coda* *(take repeat)*

D	C	G	G	

⊕ Coda

D	C	G	
I saw a were - wolf drink - in' a	pi - ña co - la - da at Trad - er Vick's;		

Outro-Chorus
w/ Loop 1

D	C	G	D	C	G	
and his hair was per - fect.			Ow - ooh!			

1. | **2.** | **Loop 1 off**

D5	C5	G5	*D5	C5	G5	
Were - wolves of Lon - don.			- don.			

*See top of first page of song for chord diagrams pertaining to rhythm slashes.

Additional Lyrics

2. You hear him howlin' around your kitchen door.
   You better not let him in!
   Little old lady got mutilated late last night;
   Werewolves of London again.

3. He's the hairy-handed gent who ran amuck in Kent;
   Lately, he's been overheard in Mayfair.
   You better stay away from him! He'll rip your lungs out, Jim!
   Huh! I'd like to meet his tailor.

4. Well, I saw Lon Chaney walking with the Queen,
   Doin' the werewolves of London.
   I saw Lon Chaney Junior walking with the Queen,
   Doin' the werewolves of London.
   I saw a werewolf drinkin' a piña colada at Trader Vick's;
   And his hair was perfect.

What It's Like

Words and Music by Erik Schrody

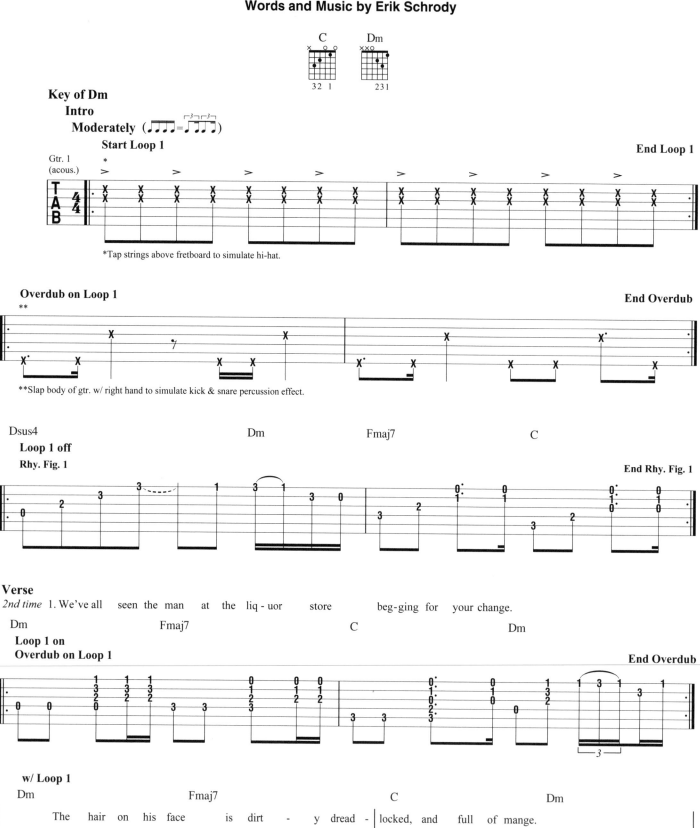

© 1998 WB MUSIC CORP. and IRISH INTELLECT MUSIC
All Rights Administered by WB MUSIC CORP.
All Rights Reserved   Used by Permission

Chorus

w/ Loop 1

Dm   Fmaj7   C   Dm

God for - bid you e - ver had to walk | a mile in his shoes

Fmaj7   C   Dm

'cause then you real - ly might know what it's like | to sing the blues.

Fmaj7   C   Dm

Then you real - ly might know what it's like. |

Fmaj7   C   Dm

Then you real - ly might know what it's like. |

Fmaj7   C   Dm

Then you real - ly might know what it's like. |

Loop 1 off

Fmaj7   *C

                                          Rhy. Fill 1   **End Rhy. Fill 1**

Then you real - ly might know what it's like. |

*See top of first page of song for chord diagrams pertaining to rhythm slashes.

𝄋 Verse

Loop 1 on

Dm   Fmaj7   C   Dm

2. Mar - y got preg-nant from a kid named Tom | that said he was in love.
3. *See additional lyrics*

Fmaj7   C   Dm

He said, "Don't wor - ry 'bout a thing, ba - by doll, I'm the man | you've been dream - ing of."

Fmaj7   C   Dm

But three months lat - er, he say he won't | date her or re - turn her calls.

Fmaj7   C   Dm

And she swear, "God damn, if I find that man | I'm cut - tin' off his balls."

Fmaj7   C   Dm

And then she heads for the clin - ic and she gets some sta | - tic walk-ing through the door.

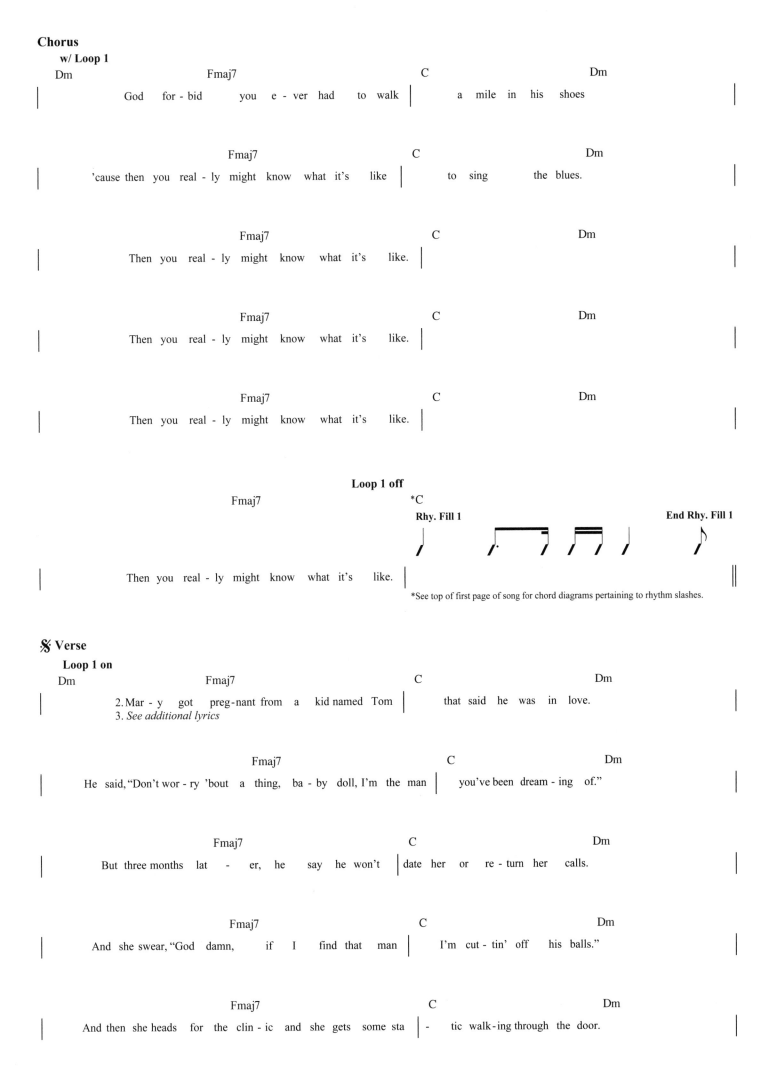

| Fmaj7 | | C | | Dm |

They call her a kil-ler, and they call her a sin-|ner, and they call her a whore.

Chorus
w/ Loop 1

Dm   Fmaj7   C   Dm

God for-bid you ev-er had to walk a mile in her shoes,

Fmaj7   C   Dm

'cause then you real-ly might know what it's like to have to choose.

Fmaj7   C   Dm

Then you real-ly might know what it's like.

Fmaj7   C   Dm

Then you real-ly might know what it's like.

To Coda ⊕

Fmaj7   C

Then you real-ly might know what it's like.

Loop 1 off **w/ Rhy. Fill 1**   **Loop 1 off**

Fmaj7   C

Then you real-ly might know what it's like.

Bridge
w/ Rhy. Fig. 1 (6 times)

Dsus4   Dm Fmaj7   C

I've seen a rich man beg. I've seen a good man sin. I've seen a tough man cry.

Dsus4   Dm Fmaj7   C

I've seen a los-er win and a sad man|grin. I heard an hon-est man lie.

Dsus4   Dm Fmaj7   C

I've seen the good side of bad and the down-side of up and ev-'ry-thing be-tween.

Dsus4   Dm Fmaj7   C

I licked the sil-ver spoon, drank from the gold-en cup and smoked the fin-est green.

Dsus4   Dm   Fmaj7   C

I stroked the fat - test dimes at least a coup - le of times   be - fore I broke their heart.

Dsus4   Dm   Fmaj7   C

You know where it ends, yo, it us - u - al - ly de - pends on where you start.

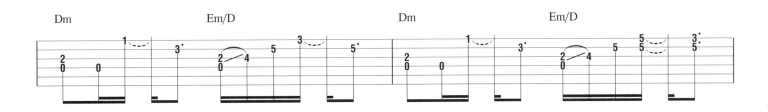

D.S. al Coda

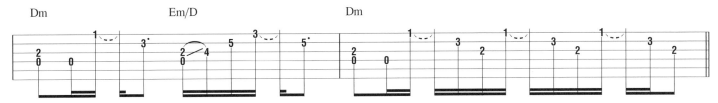

⊕ Coda

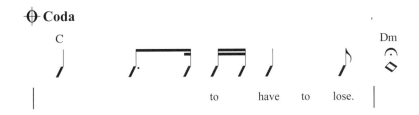

to have to lose.

Additional Lyrics

3. I knew this kid named Max who used to get fat stacks out on the corner with drugs.
He liked to hang out late; he like to get shit-faced and keep the pace with thugs.
Until late one night there was a big gun fight, and Max lost his head.
He pulled out his chrome .45, talked some shit, and wound up dead.
Now his wife and his kids are caught in the midst of all of this pain.
You know it comes that way, at least that's what they say when you play the game.

Chorus God forbid you ever had to wake up to hear the news
'Cause then you really might know what it's like to have to lose.
Then you really might know what it's like.
Then you really might know what it's like.
Then you really might know what it's like to have to lose.

Wicked Game

Words and Music by Chris Isaak

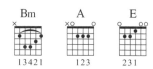

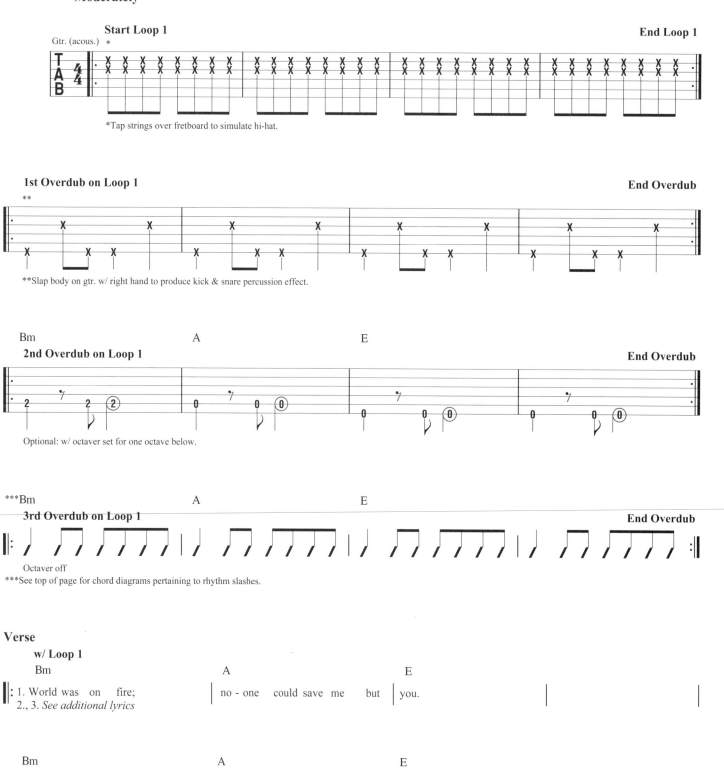

*Tap strings over fretboard to simulate hi-hat.

**Slap body on gtr. w/ right hand to produce kick & snare percussion effect.

Optional: w/ octaver set for one octave below.

Octaver off

***See top of page for chord diagrams pertaining to rhythm slashes.

Verse

w/ Loop 1

Bm	A	E	
1. World was on fire;	no-one could save me but	you.	
2., 3. *See additional lyrics*			

Bm	A	E	
Strange what de-sire will	make fool-ish peo-ple	do.	

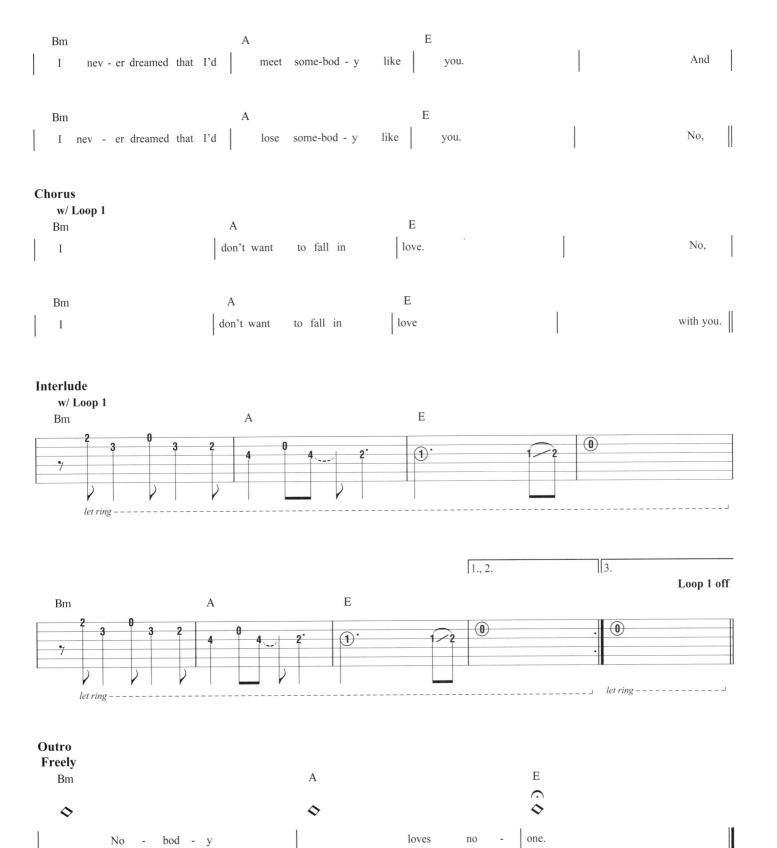

Additional Lyrics

2. What a wicked game you play to make me feel this way.
   What a wicked thing to do to let me dream of you.
   What a wicked thing to say; you never felt this way.
   What a wicked thing to do to make me dream of you.

3. World was on fire. No one could save me but you.
   Strange what desire will make foolish people do.
   I never dreamed that I'd love somebody like you.
   And I never dreamed that I'd lose somebody like you.

With or Without You

Words and Music by U2

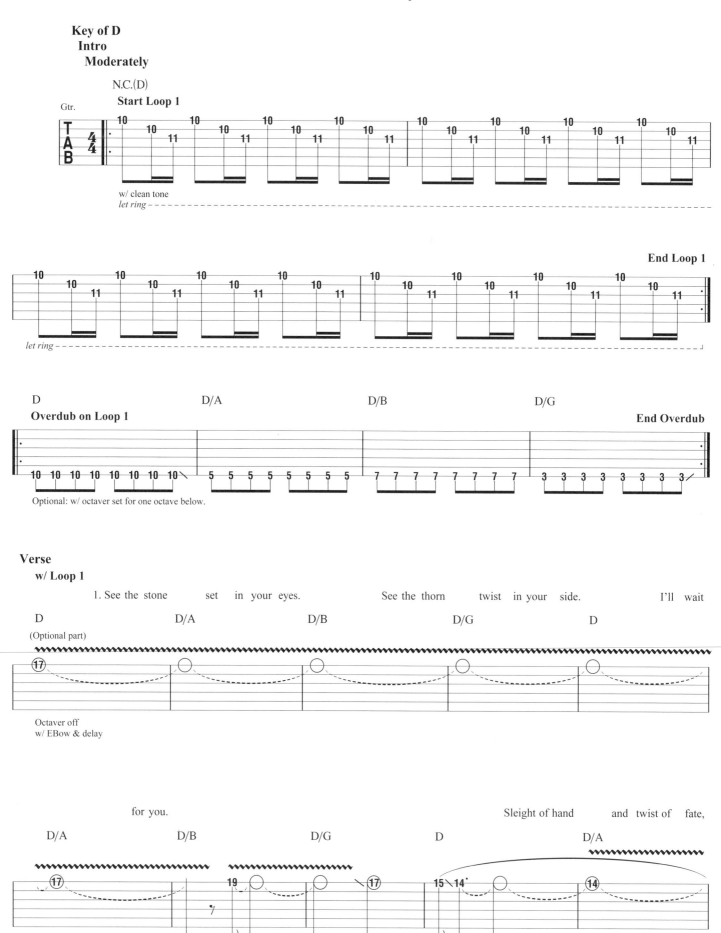

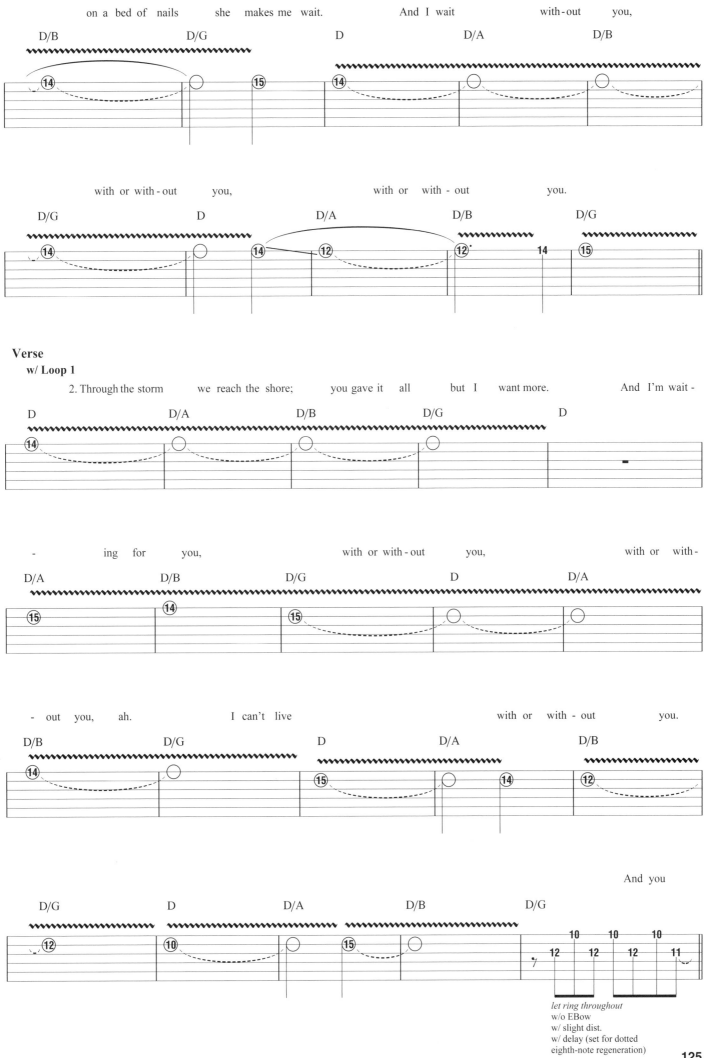

Verse
w/ Loop 1

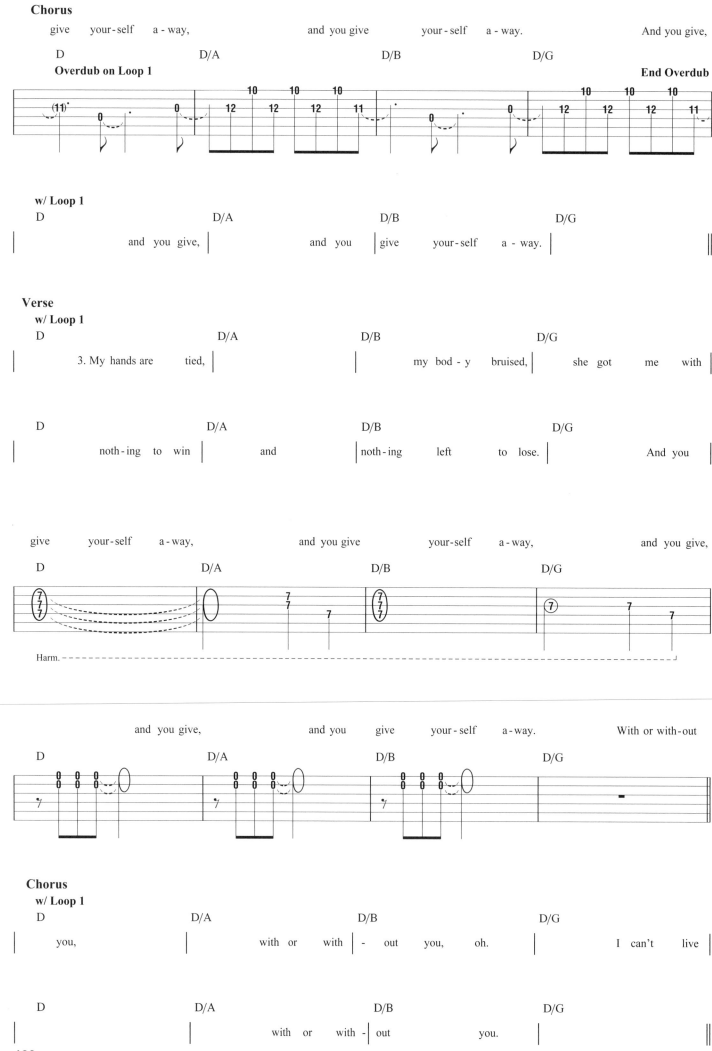

Bridge

w/ Loop 1

Whoa,   whoa.

D   D/A   D/B   D/G

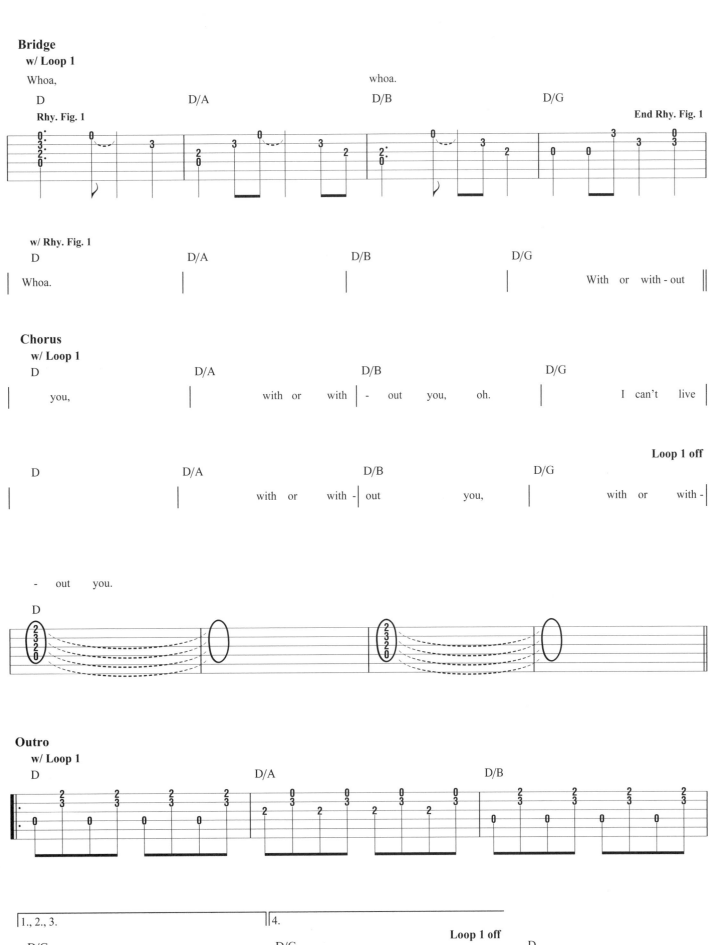

w/ Rhy. Fig. 1

D   D/A   D/B   D/G

Whoa.   With   or   with - out

Chorus

w/ Loop 1

D   D/A   D/B   D/G

you,   with or with - out you, oh.   I can't live

Loop 1 off

D   D/A   D/B   D/G

with   or   with - out   you,   with   or   with -

- out   you.

Outro

w/ Loop 1

D   D/A   D/B

1., 2., 3.   4.

Loop 1 off

D/G   D/G   D

What I Got

Words and Music by Brad Nowell, Eric Wilson, Floyd Gaugh and Lindon Roberts

D5   G5

Key of D
Intro
Moderately

N.C.
Start Loop 1

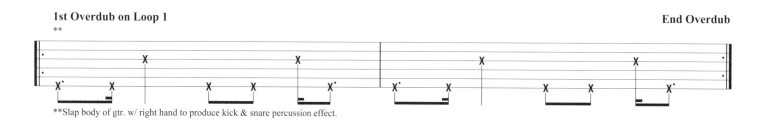

Gtr. (acous.) *

*Tap strings over fretboard to simulate hi-hat.

1st Overdub on Loop 1

End Overdub

**

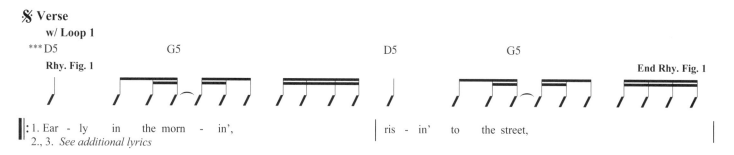

**Slap body of gtr. w/ right hand to produce kick & snare percussion effect.

D5   G5   D5   G5
2nd Overdub on Loop 1   **End Overdub**

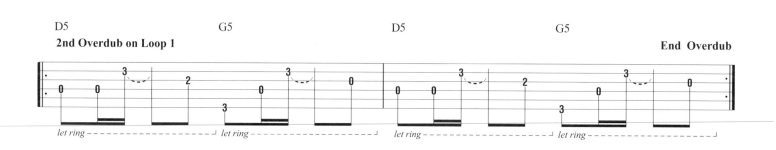

let ring - - - - - - - - - - ⌐ let ring - - - - - - - - - - ⌐ let ring - - - - - - - - - - ⌐ let ring - - - - - - - - - - ⌐

𝄋 Verse
w/ Loop 1
***D5   G5   D5   G5
Rhy. Fig. 1   **End Rhy. Fig. 1**

1. Ear - ly   in   the morn - in',   ris - in'   to   the street,
2., 3. *See additional lyrics*

***See top of page for chord diagrams pertaining to rhythm slashes.

w/ Rhy. Fig. 1 (4 1/2 times)

D5							G5			D5				G5	
light	me	up	that	cig	- a -	rette	and	I		strap	shoes	on	my	feet.	

D5					G5		D5			G5	
Got	to	find	a	rea	- son,		rea	- son things	went	wrong.	

To Coda ⊕

D5								G5	D5			G5	
Got	to	find	a	rea	- son	why	my		mon	- ey's	all	gone.	

D5			G5	D5			G5		D5		G5	
I	got	a Dal-ma	- tian,	and	I	can still get	high.		I	can play the gui	- tar like a	

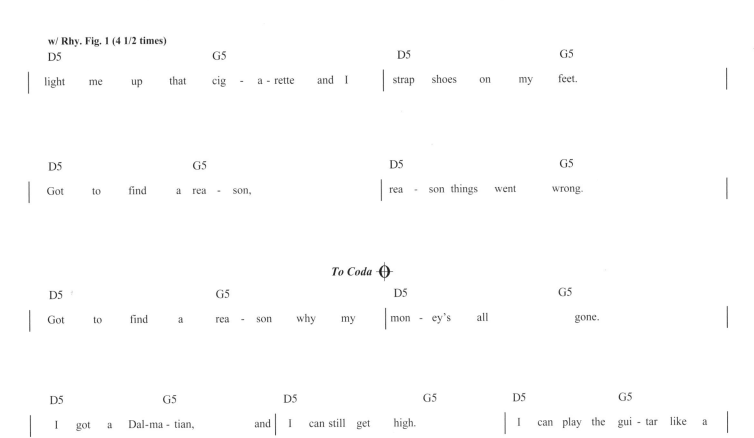

1.

Guitar Solo

moth - er - fuck - in' ri - ot.

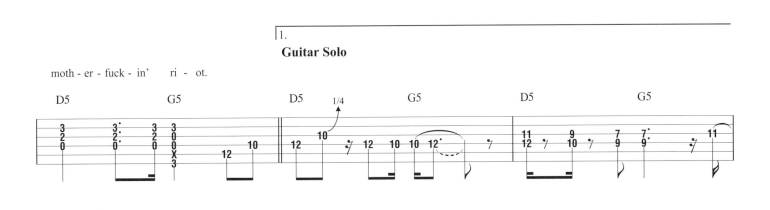

2. Well, life

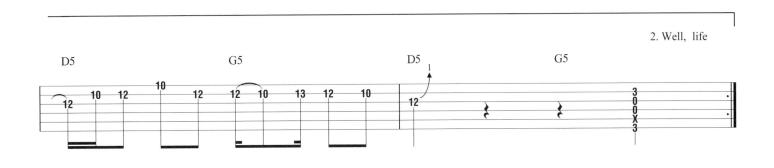

2.

Chorus

w/ Loop 1

D5					G5			D5					G5	
Lov	- in'		is	what	I	got.			I said,	re - mem - ber	that.			

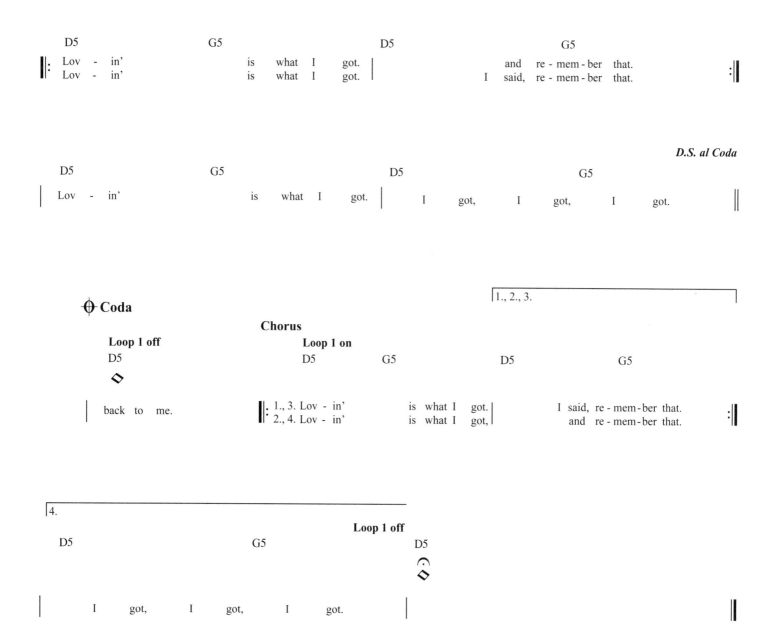

Additional Lyrics

2. Well, life is (too short) so love the one you got.
   'Cause you might get run over or you might get shot.
   Never start no static, I just get it off my (chest.)
   Never had to battle with no bullet proof (vest.)
   Take a small example, take a ti-ti-ti-tip from me,
   Take all of your money, give it all to (char-i-ty.)
   Love is what I got, it's within my reach,
   And the Sublime style's still straight from Long Beach.
   It all comes back to you, you finally get what you deserve.
   Try and test that, you're bound to get served.
   Love's what I got, don't start a riot.
   You feel it when the dance gets hot.

3. Why, I don't cry when my dog runs away.
   I don't get angry at the bills I have to pay.
   I don't get angry when my mom smokes pot,
   Hits the bottle, and goes right to the rock.
   Fuckin' and fightin', it's all the same.
   Livin' with Louie Dog's the only way to stay sane.
   Let the lovin', let the lovin' come back to me.

Yellow Ledbetter

Lyrics, as felt by Eddie Vedder
Music by Mike McCready and Jeff Ament

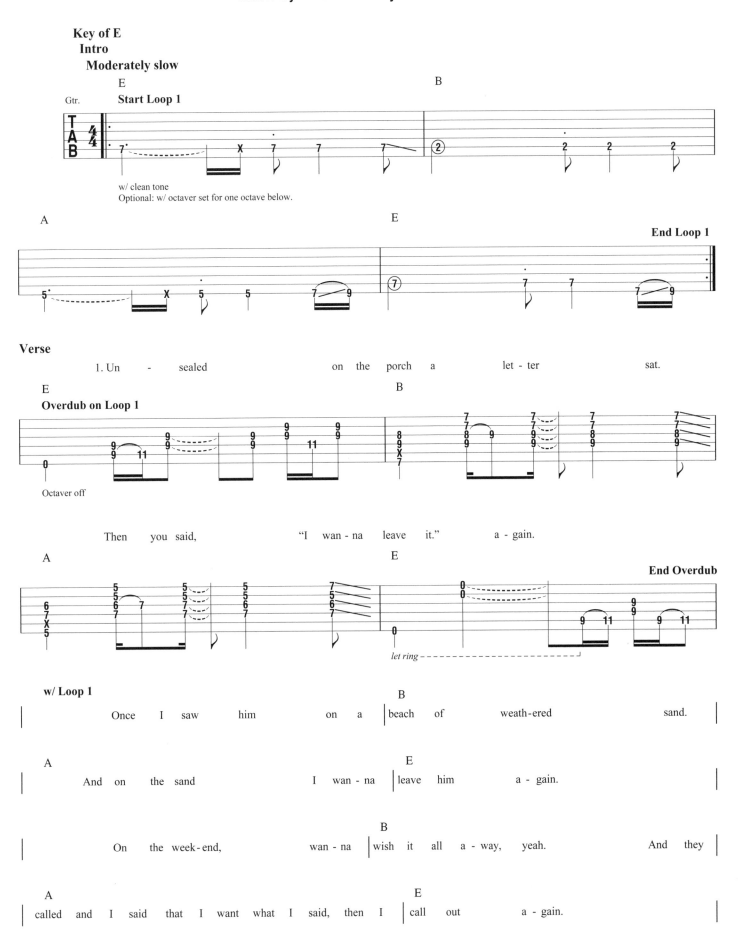

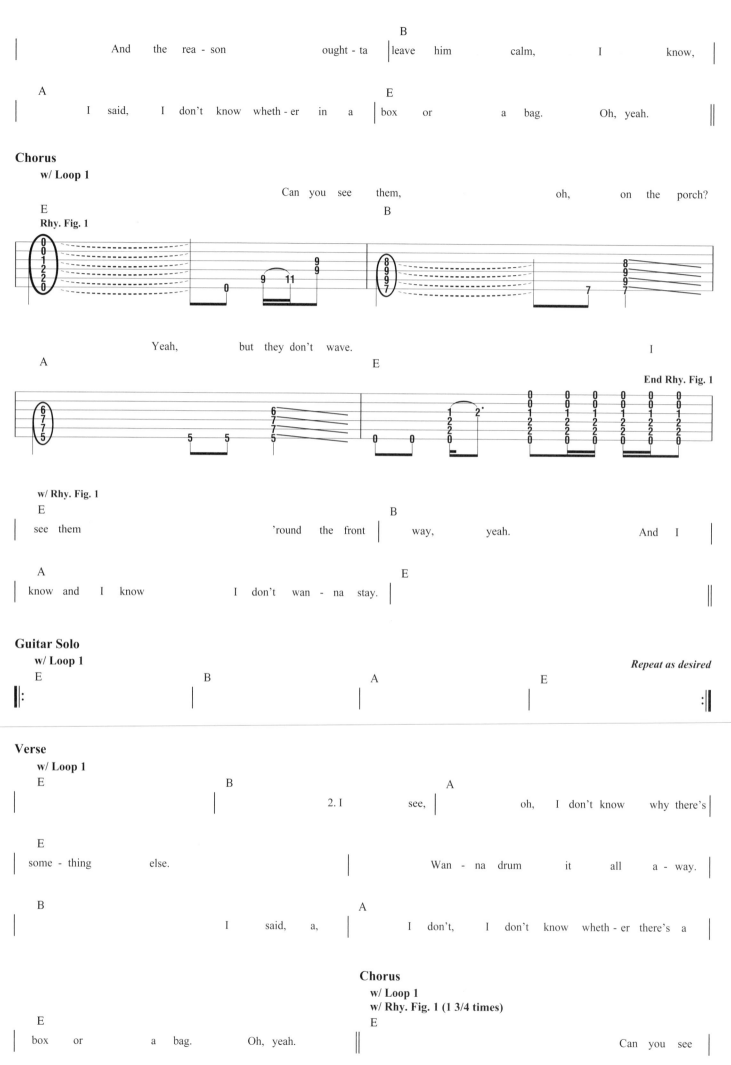

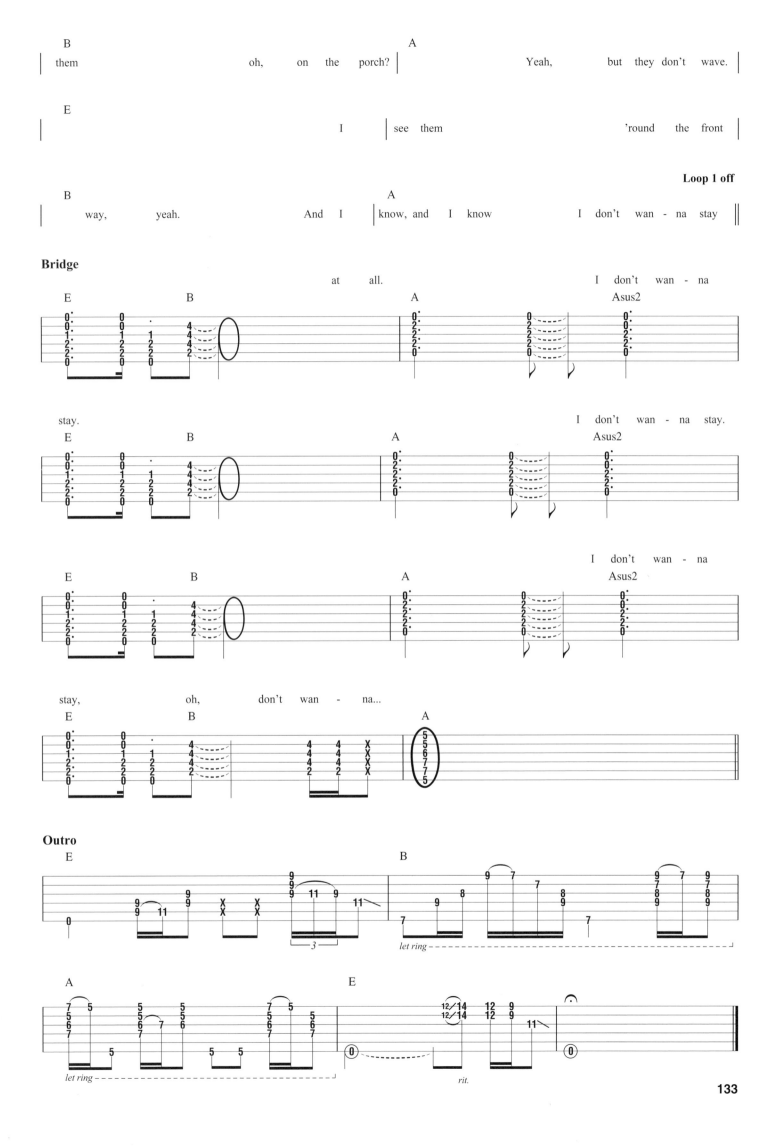

Rhythm Tab Legend

Rhythm Tab is a form of notation that adds rhythmic values to the traditional tab staff.

TABLATURE graphically represents the guitar fingerboard. Each horizontal line represents a string, and each number represents a fret. Rhythmic values are shown using ovals, stems, and dots.

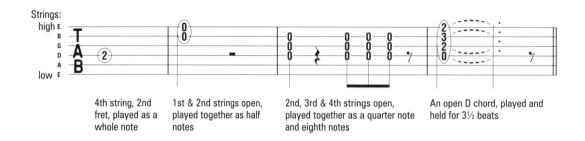

| 4th string, 2nd fret, played as a whole note | 1st & 2nd strings open, played together as half notes | 2nd, 3rd & 4th strings open, played together as a quarter note and eighth notes | An open D chord, played and held for 3½ beats |

Definitions for Special Guitar Notation

HALF-STEP BEND: Strike the note and bend up 1/2 step.

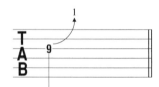

WHOLE-STEP BEND: Strike the note and bend up one step.

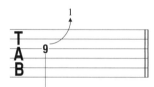

QUARTER-STEP BEND: Strike the note and bend up 1/4 step.

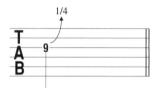

BEND AND RELEASE: Strike the note and bend up as indicated, then release back to the original note. Only the first note is struck.

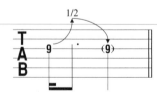

PRE-BEND: Bend the note as indicated, then strike it.

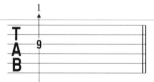

VIBRATO: The string is vibrated by rapidly bending and releasing the note with the fretting hand.

HAMMER-ON: Strike the first (lower) note with one finger, then sound the higher note (on the same string) with another finger by fretting it without picking.

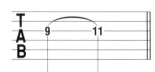

PULL-OFF: Place both fingers on the notes to be sounded. Strike the first note, and without picking, pull the finger off to sound the second (lower) note.

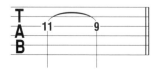

LEGATO SLIDE: Strike the first note and then slide the same fret-hand finger up or down to the second note. The second note is not struck.

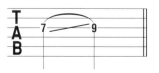

SHIFT SLIDE: Same as legato slide, except the second note is struck.

GRACE-NOTE SLUR: Strike the note and immediately hammer-on (pull-off or slide) as indicated.

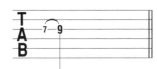

TRILL: Very rapidly alternate between the notes indicated by continuously hammering on and pulling off.

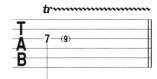

NATURAL HARMONIC: Strike the note while the fret hand lightly touches the string directly over the fret indicated.

Harm.

MUFFLED STRINGS: A percussive sound is produced by laying the fret hand across the string(s) without depressing, and striking them with the pick hand.

PALM MUTING: The note is partially muted by the pick hand lightly touching the string(s) just before the bridge.

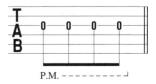

P.M. - - - - - - - - -

Additional Musical Definitions

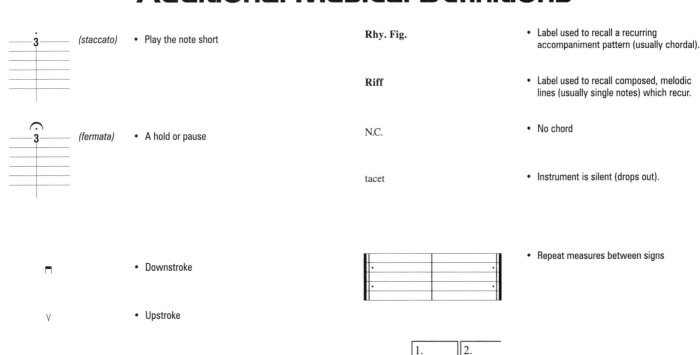

(staccato) • Play the note short

(fermata) • A hold or pause

⊓ • Downstroke

V • Upstroke

D.S. al Coda • Go back to the sign (𝄋), then play until the measure marked *"To Coda,"* then skip to the section labelled *"Coda."*

D.C. al Fine • Go back to the beginning of the song and play until the measure marked *"Fine"* (end).

Rhy. Fig. • Label used to recall a recurring accompaniment pattern (usually chordal).

Riff • Label used to recall composed, melodic lines (usually single notes) which recur.

N.C. • No chord

tacet • Instrument is silent (drops out).

• Repeat measures between signs

• When a repeated section has different endings, play the first ending only the first time and the second ending only the second time.

 • Repeat previous measure

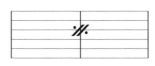 • Repeat previous two measures

NOTE: Tablature numbers in parentheses are used when:
• The note is sustained, but a new articulation begins (such as a hammer-on, pull-off, slide, or bend), or
• A bend is released.

RECORDED VERSIONS®
The Best Note-For-Note Transcriptions Available

AUTHENTIC TRANSCRIPTIONS WITH NOTES AND TABLATURE

00690603	Aerosmith – O Yeah! Ultimate Hits ...	$29.99
00690178	Alice in Chains – Acoustic	$22.99
00694865	Alice in Chains – Dirt	$22.99
00694925	Alice in Chains – Jar of Flies/Sap	$22.99
00691091	Alice Cooper – Best of	$24.99
00690958	Duane Allman – Guitar Anthology	$29.99
00694932	Allman Brothers Band – Volume 1	$29.99
00694933	Allman Brothers Band – Volume 2	$27.99
00694934	Allman Brothers Band – Volume 3	$29.99
00690945	Alter Bridge – Blackbird	$24.99
00123558	Arctic Monkeys – AM	$24.99
00214869	Avenged Sevenfold – Best of 2005-2013	$29.99
00690489	Beatles – 1	$29.99
00694929	Beatles – 1962-1966	$27.99
00694930	Beatles – 1967-1970	$29.99
00694880	Beatles – Abbey Road	$19.99
00694832	Beatles – Acoustic Guitar	$29.99
00690110	Beatles – White Album (Book 1)	$24.99
00692385	Chuck Berry	$24.99
00147787	Black Crowes – Best of	$24.99
00690149	Black Sabbath	$19.99
00690901	Black Sabbath – Best of	$22.99
00691010	Black Sabbath – Heaven and Hell	$24.99
00690148	Black Sabbath – Master of Reality	$19.99
00690142	Black Sabbath – Paranoid	$19.99
00148544	Michael Bloomfield – Guitar Anthology	$29.99
00158600	Joe Bonamassa – Blues of Desperation	$24.99
00198117	Joe Bonamassa – Muddy Wolf at Red Rocks	$24.99
00283540	Joe Bonamassa – Redemption	$24.99
00358863	Joe Bonamassa – Royal Tea	$24.99
00690913	Boston	$22.99
00690491	David Bowie – Best of	$24.99
00286503	Big Bill Broonzy – Guitar Collection	$19.99
00690261	The Carter Family Collection	$19.99
00691079	Johnny Cash – Best of	$24.99
00690936	Eric Clapton – Complete Clapton	$34.99
00694869	Eric Clapton – Unplugged	$26.99
00124873	Eric Clapton – Unplugged (Deluxe)	$29.99
00138731	Eric Clapton & Friends – The Breeze	$24.99
00389392	Gary Clark Jr. – Anthology	$29.99
00139967	Coheed & Cambria – In Keeping Secrets of Silent Earth: 3	$24.99
00141704	Jesse Cook – Works, Vol. 1	$22.99
00288787	Creed – Greatest Hits	$22.99
00690819	Creedence Clearwater Revival	$27.99
00690648	Jim Croce – Very Best of	$22.99
00690572	Steve Cropper – Soul Man	$22.99
00690613	Crosby, Stills & Nash – Best of	$29.99
00690784	Def Leppard – Best of	$24.99
00694831	Derek and the Dominos – Layla & Other Assorted Love Songs	$24.99
00291164	Dream Theater – Distance Over Time	$24.99
00278631	Eagles – Greatest Hits 1971-1975	$22.99
00278632	Eagles – Very Best of	$39.99
00690515	Extreme II – Pornograffiti	$24.99
00150257	John Fahey – Guitar Anthology	$24.99
00690664	Fleetwood Mac – Best of	$24.99
00691024	Foo Fighters – Greatest Hits	$24.99
00120220	Robben Ford – Guitar Anthology	$29.99
00295410	Rory Gallagher – Blues	$24.99
00139460	Grateful Dead – Guitar Anthology	$34.99
00691190	Peter Green – Best of	$24.99

00287517	Greta Van Fleet – Anthem of the Peaceful Army	$22.99
00287515	Greta Van Fleet – From the Fires	$24.99
00369065	Greta Van Fleet – The Battle At Garden's Gate	$24.99
00694798	George Harrison – Anthology	$24.99
00692930	Jimi Hendrix – Are You Experienced?	$29.99
00692931	Jimi Hendrix – Axis: Bold As Love	$24.99
00690304	Jimi Hendrix – Band of Gypsys	$27.99
00694944	Jimi Hendrix – Blues	$29.99
00692932	Jimi Hendrix – Electric Ladyland	$29.99
00660029	Buddy Holly – Best of	$24.99
00200446	Iron Maiden – Guitar Tab	$34.99
00694912	Eric Johnson – Ah Via Musicom	$24.99
00690271	Robert Johnson – Transcriptions	$27.99
00690427	Judas Priest – Best of	$24.99
00690492	B.B. King – Anthology	$29.99
00130447	B.B. King – Live at the Regal	$19.99
00690134	Freddie King – Collection	$22.99
00327968	Marcus King – El Dorado	$22.99
00690157	Kiss – Alive	$19.99
00690356	Kiss – Alive II	$24.99
00291163	Kiss – Very Best of	$29.99
00345767	Greg Koch – Best of	$29.99
00690377	Kris Kristofferson – Guitar Collection	$22.99
00690834	Lamb of God – Ashes of the Wake	$24.99
00690525	George Lynch – Best of	$29.99
00690955	Lynyrd Skynyrd – All-Time Greatest Hits	$24.99
00694954	Lynyrd Skynyrd – New Best of	$27.99
00690577	Yngwie Malmsteen – Anthology	$29.99
00694896	John Mayall with Eric Clapton – Blues Breakers	$22.99
00694952	Megadeth – Countdown to Extinction	$24.99
00276065	Megadeth – Greatest Hits: Back to the Start	$27.99
00694951	Megadeth – Rust in Peace	$29.99
00690011	Megadeth – Youthanasia	$24.99
00209876	Metallica – Hardwired to Self-Destruct	$29.99
00690646	Pat Metheny – One Quiet Night	$27.99
00102591	Wes Montgomery – Guitar Anthology	$29.99
00691092	Gary Moore – Best of	$27.99
00694802	Gary Moore – Still Got the Blues	$24.99
00355456	Alanis Morisette – Jagged Little Pill	$22.99
00690611	Nirvana	$24.99
00694913	Nirvana – In Utero	$22.99
00694883	Nirvana – Nevermind	$22.99
00690026	Nirvana – Unplugged in New York	$22.99
00265439	Nothing More – Tab Collection	$24.99
00243349	Opeth – Best of	$22.99
00690499	Tom Petty – Definitive Guitar Collection	$24.99
00121933	Pink Floyd – Acoustic Guitar Collection	$29.99
00690428	Pink Floyd – Dark Side of the Moon	$22.99
00244637	Pink Floyd – Guitar Anthology	$24.99
00239799	Pink Floyd – The Wall	$27.99
00690789	Poison – Best of	$22.99
00690925	Prince – Very Best of	$24.99
00690003	Queen – Classic Queen	$26.99
00694975	Queen – Greatest Hits	$27.99
00694910	Rage Against the Machine	$24.99
00119834	Rage Against the Machine – Guitar Anthology	$24.99
00690426	Ratt – Best of	$24.99

00690055	Red Hot Chili Peppers – Blood Sugar Sex Magik	$19.99
00690379	Red Hot Chili Peppers – Californication	$22.99
00690673	Red Hot Chili Peppers – Greatest Hits	$24.99
01120374	Red Hot Chili Peppers – Return of the Dream Canteen	$29.99
00690852	Red Hot Chili Peppers – Stadium Arcadium	$29.99
00706518	Red Hot Chili Peppers – Unlimited Love	$27.99
00690511	Django Reinhardt – Definitive Collection	$24.99
00690014	Rolling Stones – Exile on Main Street	$24.99
00690631	Rolling Stones – Guitar Anthology	$34.99
00323854	Rush – The Spirit of Radio: Greatest Hits, 1974-1987	$26.99
00173534	Santana – Guitar Anthology	$29.99
00276350	Joe Satriani – What Happens Next	$24.99
00690566	Scorpions – Best of	$26.99
00690604	Bob Seger – Guitar Collection	$24.99
00234543	Ed Sheeran – Divide*	$22.99
00691114	Slash – Guitar Anthology	$34.99
00690813	Slayer – Guitar Collection	$24.99
00690419	Slipknot	$22.99
00316982	Smashing Pumpkins – Greatest Hits	$24.99
00690912	Soundgarden – Guitar Anthology	$26.99
00120004	Steely Dan – Best of	$27.99
00322564	Stone Temple Pilots – Thank You	$26.99
00690520	Styx – Guitar Collection	$24.99
00120081	Sublime	$22.99
00690531	System of a Down – Toxicity	$19.99
00694824	James Taylor – Best of	$22.99
00694887	Thin Lizzy – Best of	$22.99
00253237	Trivium – Guitar Tab Anthology	$24.99
00690683	Robin Trower – Bridge of Sighs	$19.99
00156024	Steve Vai – Guitar Anthology	$39.99
00419534	Steve Vai – Inviolate	$29.99
00660137	Steve Vai – Passion & Warfare	$29.99
00295076	Van Halen – 30 Classics	$29.99
00690024	Stevie Ray Vaughan – Couldn't Stand the Weather	$22.99
00660058	Stevie Ray Vaughan – Lightnin' Blues 1983-1987	$29.99
00217455	Stevie Ray Vaughan – Plays Slow Blues	$24.99
00694835	Stevie Ray Vaughan – The Sky Is Crying	$24.99
00690015	Stevie Ray Vaughan – Texas Flood	$22.99
00694789	Muddy Waters – Deep Blues	$27.99
00152161	Doc Watson – Guitar Anthology	$26.99
00690071	Weezer (The Blue Album)	$22.99
00237811	White Stripes – Greatest Hits	$24.99
00117511	Whitesnake – Guitar Collection	$24.99
00122303	Yes – Guitar Collection	$24.99
00690443	Frank Zappa – Hot Rats	$22.99
00121684	ZZ Top – Early Classics	$27.99
00690589	ZZ Top – Guitar Anthology	$27.99

COMPLETE SERIES LIST ONLINE!

HAL•LEONARD®
www.halleonard.com

Prices and availability subject to change without notice.
*Tab transcriptions only.

0423
272